# THE MANUFACTURING OF GRETA THUNBERG

CORY MORNINGSTAR

A world of gratitude to the following people:

Forrest Palmer, Wrong Kind of Green Collective (first edit)

Geraldine Ring, Activist (final edit)

Jenn Laskin (synopsis)

Boris Forkel (Editor)

Constance Wren, Illustrator, Cover

Professor Tim Hayward

Professor Clive Spash

Patrick Farnsworth, Last Born in the Wilderness

Brian Davey, Activist, Feasta

John Steppling, Author/Playwright

Hiroyuki Hamada, Artist

Prolekult Films

Teko Alejo, Michael Swifte, and so many others who have supported and shared my work. Thank you for your courage, insights, and knowledge.

May we fight until the bitter end.

+++

Respect and love to those closest to me, my partner and my children, who I love fiercely.

Bibliografische Information der Deutschen Nationalbibliothek:
Die Deutsche Nationalbibliothek verzeichnet diese Publikation in der Deutschen Nationalbibliografie; detaillierte bibliografische Daten sind im Internet unter http://dnb.dnb.de abrufbar.

The Manufacturing of Greta Thunberg

Herstellung und Verlag: BoD – Books on Demand, Norderstedt.

ISBN: 9783749464753
BabylonApocalypse.org

FSC
www.fsc.org
MIX
Papier aus verantwortungsvollen Quellen
Paper from responsible sources
FSC® C105338

*"What's infuriating about manipulations by the Non Profit Industrial Complex is that they harvest the goodwill of the people, especially young people. They target those who were not given the skills and knowledge to truly think for themselves by institutions which are designed to serve the ruling class. Capitalism operates systematically and structurally like a cage to raise domesticated animals. Those organizations and their projects which operate under false slogans of humanity in order to prop up the hierarchy of money and violence are fast becoming some of the most crucial elements of the invisible cage of corporatism, colonialism and militarism." Hiroyuki Hamada, artist*

1958: "17-year-old Bianca Passarge of Hamburg dresses up as a cat, complete with furry tail, and dances on wine bottles. Her performance was based on a dream and she practiced for eight hours every day in order to perfect her dance."

## THE MANUFACTURING OF GRETA THUNBERG – FOR CONSENT HAS BEEN WRITTEN IN SIX ACTS

In **ACT I**, I disclose that Greta Thunberg, the current child prodigy and face of the youth movement to combat climate change, serves as special youth advisor and trustee to the foundation established by "We Don't Have Time", a burgeoning mainstream tech start-up. I then explore the ambitions behind We Don't Have Time.

In **ACT II**, I illustrate how today's youth are the sacrificial lambs for the ruling elite. Also in this act, I introduce the board members of and advisors to We Don't Have Time. I explore the leadership in the nascent We Don't Have Time and the partnerships between the well-established corporate environmental entities: Al Gore's Climate Reality Project, 350.org, Avaaz, Global Utmaning (Global Challenge), the World Bank, and the World Economic Forum (WEF).

In **ACT III**, I deconstruct how Al Gore and the planet's most powerful capitalists are behind today's manufactured youth movements and why. I explore the We Don't Have Time/Thunberg connections to Our Revolution, the Sanders Institute, This Is Zero Hour, the Sunrise Movement and the Green New Deal. I also touch upon Thunberg's famous family. In particular, Thunberg's celebrity mother, Malena Ernman (WWF Environmental Hero of the Year 2017) and her August 2018 book launch. I then explore the generous media attention afforded to Thunberg in both May and April of 2018 by SvD, one of Sweden's largest newspapers.

In **ACT IV**, I examine the current campaign, now unfolding, in "leading the public into emergency mode". More importantly, I summarize who and what this mode is to serve.

In **ACT V**, I take a closer look at the Green New Deal. I explore Data for Progress and the targeting of female youth as a key "femographic". I connect the primary architect and authors of the "Green New Deal" data to the World Resources Institute. From there, I walk you through the interlocking Business & Sustainable Development Commission, the global Commission on the Economy and Climate, and the New Climate Economy – a project of the World Resources Institute. I disclose the common thread between these groups and the assignment of money to nature, represented by the Natural Capital Coalition and the non-profit industrial complex as an entity. Finally, I reveal how this has culminated in the implementation of payments for ecosystem services (the financialization and privatization of nature, global in scale) which is "expected to be adopted during the fifteenth meeting in Beijing in 2020."

In the final act, **ACT VI** [Crescendo], I wrap up the series by divulging that the very foundations which have financed the climate "movement" over the past decade are the same foundations now partnered with the Climate Finance Partnership looking to unlock 100 trillion dollars from pension funds. I reveal the identities of individuals and groups at the helm of this interlocking matrix, controlling both the medium and the message. I take a step back in time to briefly demonstrate the ten years of strategic social engineering that have brought us to this very precipice. I look at the relationship between WWF, Stockholm Institute and World Resources Institute as key instruments in the creation of the financialization of nature. I also take a look at the first public campaigns for the financialization of nature ("natural capital") that are slowly being brought into the public realm by WWF. I reflect upon how mainstream NGOs are attempting to safeguard their influence and further manipulate the populace by going underground through Extinction Rebellion groups being organized in the US and across the world.

With the smoke now cleared, the weak and essentially non-existent demands reminiscent of the 2009 TckTckTck "demands" can now be fully understood.[1]

Some of these topics, in addition to others, will be released and discussed in further detail as addenda built on the large volume of research. This includes stepping through the looking glass, with an exploration of what the real "Green New Deal" under the Fourth Industrial Revolution will look like. Also forthcoming is a look at the power of celebrity – and how it has become a key tool for both capital and conformity.

1 Note: This series contains information and quotes that have been translated from Swedish to English via Google Translate.

## TABLE OF CONTENTS

# ACT I

## THE POLITICAL ECONOMY OF THE NON-PROFIT INDUSTRIAL COMPLEX

*"How is it possible for you to be so easily tricked by something so simple as a story, because you are tricked? Well, it all comes down to one core thing and that is **emotional investment.** The more emotionally invested you are in anything in your life, the less critical and the less objectively observant you become."*
*— David JP Phillips, We Don't Have Time board of directors, "The Magical Science of Storytelling"*

Oktober 26, 2018, Facebook: Thunberg, We Don't Have Time

August 2018, Finance Monthly: co-founder of We Don't Have Time, Ingmar Rentzhog

## WE DON'T HAVE TIME

As this term is quickly becoming the quote du jour as a collective mantra to address the ongoing environmental disaster that can best be described as a nod to the obvious, it's true that we don't have time. We don't have time to stop imperialist wars – wars being the greatest contributor to climate change and environmental degradation by far – but we must do so. Of course this is an impossible feat under the crushing weight of the capitalist system, a US war economy, and the push for a fourth industrial revolution founded on renewable energy. Yet, inconvenience has nothing to do with necessity in regards to addressing a particular situation. What is never discussed in regards to the so-called "clean energy revolution" is that its existence is wholly dependent on "green" imperialism – the latter term being synonymous with blood.

But that's not what this series is about.

This series is about new financial markets in a world where global economic growth is experiencing stagnation. The threat – and subsequent response – is not so much about climate change as it is about the collapse of the capitalist economic system. This series is about the climate wealth opportunity of unprecedented growth, profits, and the measures our elite classes will take in order to achieve it – including the exploitation of the youth.

## WHAT IS WE DON'T HAVE TIME?

> *"Our goal is to become among the biggest players on the internet." — Ingmar Rentzhog, We Don't Have Time, December 22, 2017, Nordic Business Insider*[2]

On August 20, 2018, a tweet[3] featuring a photo of "a Swedish girl" sitting on a sidewalk was released by the tech company We Don't Have Time, founded by its CEO Ingmar Rentzhog:

> *"One 15 year old girl in front of the Swedish parliament is striking from School until Election Day in 3 weeks[.] Imagine how lonely she must feel in this picture. People where [sic] just walking by. Continuing with the business as usual thing. But the truth is. We can't and she knows it!"*

Rentzhog's tweet, via the We Don't Have Time Twitter account, would be the very first exposure of Thunberg's now famous school strike.

Above: "We Don't Have Time" tweet, August 20, 2018

Ingmar Rentzhog, Årets Miljöinfluencer 2018.

Tagged in Rentzhog's "lonely girl" tweet were five Twitter accounts: Greta Thunberg, Zero Hour (youth movement), Jamie Margolin (the teenage founder of Zero Hour), Al Gore's Climate Reality Project, and the People's Climate Strike Twitter account (in the identical font and aesthetics as 350.org). [These groups will be touched upon briefly later in this series.]

2 https://nordic.businessinsider.com/this-swedish-crowdfunding-project-is-riffing-off-metoo-to-save-the-climate--/
3 https://twitter.com/WeDontHaveTime0/status/1031657287763599365

Rentzhog is the founder of Laika (a prominent Swedish communications consultancy firm providing services to the financial industry, recently acquired by FundedByMe). He was appointed chair of the think tank Global Utmaning (Global Challenge in English) on May 24, 2018,[4] and serves on the board of FundedByMe.[5] Rentzhog is a member of Al Gore's Climate Reality Organization Leaders, where he is part of the European Climate Policy Task Force. He received his training in March 2017 from former US Vice President Al Gore in Denver, USA, and again in June 2018, in Berlin.

Founded in 2006, Al Gore's Climate Reality Project is a partner of We Don't Have Time.

The We Don't Have Time Foundation cites two special youth advisors and trustees: Greta Thunberg and Jamie Margolin.[6]

Mårten Thorslund, chief marketing and sustainability officer of We Don't Have Time, took many of the very first photos of Thunberg following the launch of her school strike on August 20, 2018. In the following instance, photos taken by Thorslund accompany the article written by David Olsson, chief operating officer of We Don't Have Time, *This 15-year-old Girl Breaks Swedish Law for the Climate,* published August 23, 2018:[7]

> *"Greta became a climate champion and tried to influence those closest to her. Her father now writes articles and gives lectures on the climate crisis, whereas her mother, a famous Swedish opera singer, has stopped flying. All thanks to Greta.*
>
> *And clearly, she has stepped up her game, influencing the national conversation on the climate crisis — two weeks before the election.* ***We Don't Have Time reported on Greta's strike on its first day*** *and in less than 24 hours our Facebook posts and tweets received over twenty thousand likes, shares and comments. It didn't take long for national media to catch on. As of the first week of the strike,* ***at least six major daily newspapers****, as well as Swedish and Danish national TV,[8] have interviewed Greta.*

4 https://www.globalutmaning.se/ingmar-rentzhog-ny-ordforande-global-utmaning/
5 https://www.ilovefundedbyme.com/
6 https://wedonthavetime.org/launch/about/
7 https://medium.com/wedonthavetime/this-15-year-old-girl-breaks-swedish-law-for-the-climate-d1a48ab97e3a
8 TV 2 Danmark Danish public service, SVT Swedish public service, TV 4 News, Metro TV, Dagens Nyheter, Aftonbladet(August 20, 2018), Sydsvenskan, Stockholm Direkt, Expressen (August 20, 2018) , ETC, WWF, Effekt Magazin, GöteborgsPosten,Helsingborgs Dagblad, Folkbladet, Uppsala Nya tidning, Vimmerby Tidning, Piteå Tidningen, Borås Tidning, Duggan, VT, NT, Corren, OMNI, WeDontHaveTime CEO viral FaceBook post that mention it first.[https://medium.com/wedonthavetime/this-15-year-old-girl-breaks-swedish-law-for-the-climate-d1a48ab97e3a]

*Two Swedish party leaders have stopped by to talk to her as well." [Emphasis added]*

The article continues:

> *"Is there something big going on here? This* ***one kid*** *immediately got twenty supporters who now sit next to her. This* ***one kid*** *created numerous news stories in national newspapers and on TV. This* ***one kid*** *has received thousands of messages of love and support on social media.... Movements by young people, such as Jaime Margolin's #ThisIsZeroHour that #WeDontHaveTime interviewed earlier, speaks with a much needed urgency that grown-ups should pay attention to..." [Emphasis in original]*

Yes – there was, and still is, something going on.

It's called marketing and branding.

> *"Yesterday I sat completely by myself, today there is one other here too. There are none [that] I know." — Greta Thunberg, August 21, 2018, Nyheter newspaper, Sweden[9] [Translation via Google]*

The "one kid immediately got twenty supporters" – from a Swedish network for sustainable business. What is going on – is the launch of a global campaign to usher in a required consensus for the Paris Agreement, the Green New Deal and all climate-related policies and legislation written by the power elite – for the power elite. This is necessary in order to unlock the trillions of dollars in funding by way of massive public demand.

These agreements and policies include carbon capture and storage (CCS), enhanced oil recovery (EOR), bio-energy with carbon capture and storage (BECCS), rapid total decarbonization, payments for ecosystem services (referred to as "natural capital"), nuclear energy and fission and a host of other "solutions" that are hostile to an already devastated planet. What is going on – is a rebooting of a stagnant capitalist economy – that needs new markets, new growth – in order to save itself. What is being created is a mechanism to unlock approximately 90 trillion dollars[10] for new investments and infrastructure. What is going on is the creation of, and investment in, perhaps the biggest behavioural change experiment yet attempted, global in scale. And what are the deciding factors in what behaviours global society should adhere to? And more

9 https://www.svt.se/nyheter/lokalt/stockholm/greta-thunberg-15-klimatfragan-ar-var-tids-odesfraga
10 https://www.fastcompany.com/90230359/fighting-climate-change-could-boost-the-global-economy-by-26-trillion

importantly, who decides? This is a rhetorical question, as we know full well the answer: the same Western white male saviours and the capitalist economic system they have implemented globally that has been the cause of our planetary ecological nightmare. This crisis continues unabated as they appoint themselves (yet again) as the saviours for all humanity – a recurring problem for centuries.

*"Our goal is to become at least 100 million users. It is an eighth of all who have climbed on social media. Only last month we managed to reach 18 million social media accounts according to a media survey that Meltwater news made for us. At Facebook, we are currently seven times the number of followers among the world's all climate organizations. We are growing with 10,000 new global followers per day on Facebook." — Ingmar Rentzhog interview with Miljö & Utveckling, October 15, 2018*[11]

We Don't Have Time identifies itself as a movement and tech-startup that is currently developing "the world's largest social network for climate action". The "movement" component was launched on April 22, 2018. The web platform is still in the progress of being built[12], but is to launch on April 22, 2019 (coinciding with Earth Day). "Through our platform, millions of members will unite to put pressure on leaders, politicians and corporations to act for the climate." The start-up's goal to rapidly achieve 100 million users has thus far attracted 435 investors[13] (74.52% of the company's shares) via the web platform FundedByMe.

The start-up intends to offer partnerships, digital advertising and services related to climate change, sustainability and the growing green, circular economy to "a large audience of engaged consumers and ambassadors."

We Don't Have Time is mainly active in three markets: social media, digital advertising and carbon offsets. ["In the US alone, estimated market for carbon offsetting amount to over 82 billion USD of which voluntary carbon offset represents 191 million USD. The market is expected to increase in the future, in 2019, an estimated 15% of all greenhouse gas emissions will be associated with any kind of cost for offsetting."]

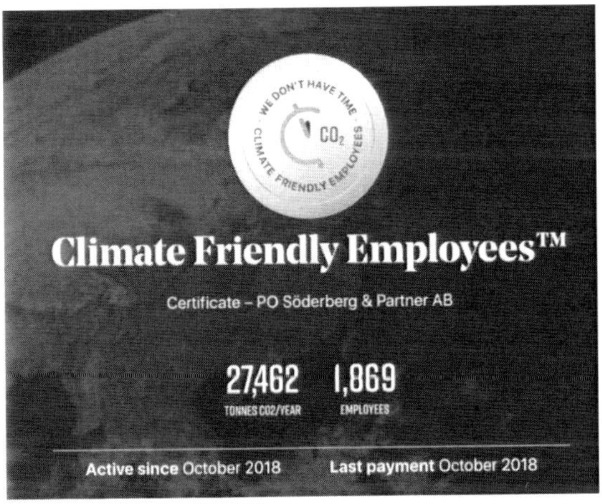


As the company is a niche orgsanization, social networks are able to provide services tailored to platform users. The start-up has identified such an opportunity by offering its

11 https://miljo-utveckling.se/ingmar-rentzhog-ar-arets-miljoinfluencer-2018/
12 https://wedonthavetime.org/launch/
13 https://www.fundedbyme.com/sv/campaign/8227/we-dont-have-time/

users the ability to purchase carbon offsets through the platform's own certification. This option applies to both the individual users of the platform, as well as to whole organizations/companies on the platform.

One incentive of many identified in the start-up investment section[14] is that users will be encouraged to "communicate jointly and powerfully with influential actors." Such influencers are Greta Thunberg and Jamie Margolin who both have lucrative futures in the branding of "sustainable" industries and products, should they wish to pursue this path in utilizing their present celebrity for personal gain (a hallmark of the "grassroots" NGO movement).

The tech company is banking on creating a massive member base of "conscious users" that will enable "profitable commercial collaborations, for example, advertising":

> *"Decision makers – politicians, companies, organizations, states – get a **climate rating** based on their ability to live up to the users' initiative. Knowledge and opinion gather in one place and users put pressure on decision makers to drive a faster change."*

> *"The main sources of revenue come from commercial players who have received high climate rating and confidence in the We Don't Have Times member base.[15]... **The revenue model will resemble the social platform of TripAdvisor.com's business model, which with its 390 million users annually generates over $ 1 billion in good profitability**...**We will work with strategic partners such as Climate Reality leaders, climate organizations, bloggers, influencers and leading experts in the field**."*

A "state of conscious and permanent visibility assures the automatic functioning of power." — *Michel Foucault's Discipline and Punish*

Comparable to other social media endeavors where "likes", "followers" and unfathomable amounts of metadata determine financial success, the fact that the business is virtual enables high profit margins. The return on investment,[16] best described as mainstream acquiescence and desirability by way of exposure, will be obtained through future dividends. In anticipation of this pro-

14 https://www.fundedbyme.com/sv/campaign/8227/we-dont-have-time/

15 Click-based advertising based on highly rated companies that want to drive traffic to their websites; Targeted web advertising for companies that want to reach out to environmentally aware users in different segments; Business subscriptions where companies and organizations have the opportunity to interact with the members and get the right to use the We Don't Have Times brand and the company's rating in their marketing [https://www.fundedbyme.com/sv/campaign/8227/we-dont-have-time/]

16 https://www.fundedbyme.com/sv/campaign/8227/we-dont-have-time/#return-on-investment

jected success, the tech company plans to take its business to the stock exchange in the near future (think Facebook and Instagram). The most critical component to the success of this start-up (like its predecessors) is achieving a massive member base. Therefore, according to the company, it "will work actively with both enlisting influencers and creating content for various campaigns linked to the hashtag #WeDontHaveTime."

On April 18, 2018, the crowdfunding platform FundedByMe (utilized by We Don't Have Time to enlist investors) acquired Ingmar Rentzhog's Laika Consulting. Excerpts from the press release are as follows:

> *"FundedByMe today announced that they acquire 100% of the shares in the established financial company* ***Laika Consulting AB, a leading communications agency in financial communications. As a result, the company doubles its investment network to close to 250,000 members, making it the largest in the Nordic region.*** *The acquisition is a strategic step to further strengthen FundedByMe's range of financial services...*
>
> ***[Ingmar Rentzhog] will continue to work on strategic client projects*** *for FundedByMe and Laika Consulting*[17] *in part-time. Moreover he takes a role in the company's board.* ***The majority of his time he will focus on climate change through the newly established company, "We Don't Have Time", as a CEO and founder****."*[18]*[Emphasis added]*

17 "Laika Consulting was one of the first companies in Sweden to work with crowdfunding when we established the brand in 2004. I look forward to follow the company's growth closely. A combination of Laika's expertise in listed companies, together with FundedByMe with its international and digital presence, can create new opportunities for growth."says Laika's CEO, Ingmar Rentzhog."

18 http://news.cision.com/fundedbyme/r/fundedbyme-acquires-laika-consulting,c2500454

## WE DON'T HAVE TIME SOFTWARE APP: THE LATEST WAVE OF WESTERN & CORPORATE IDEOLOGY AT YOUR FINGER-TIPS

In October 2016, Netflix aired the third season of Black Mirror, "a Twilight Zone–esque anthology TV series about technological anxieties and possible futures." The first episode "Nosedive" posits a shallow and hypocritical populace in which "social platforms, self-curation and validation-seeking" have become the underpinning of a future society. [Black Mirror's third season opens with a vicious take on social media.] The disturbing episode shares parallels to the concept behind We Don't Have Time. The difference being instead of rating people exclusively, we will be rating brands, products, corporations and everything else climate related.

AI Magazine Issue 10 2018 | pages: 8 / 78

rally around a cause, our system will be designed to highlight this and prompt businesses, politicians and other leaders to act. If, for instance, 500 users object to the use of plastic bags in a local convenience store, the manager of that store will receive an automatically generated email from the platform and the store's overall We Don't Have Time rating will be negatively affected. However, if the store goes on to do something about it, our users will appreciate this and improve the store's rating.

Acquisition International Magazine Issue 10, 2018

The not unintended results will be tenfold. The corporations with the best advertising executives and largest budgets will be the winners. Greenwashing will become an unprecedented method of advertising as will the art of "storytelling" (no one ever said a story has to be true). Small or local businesses with little financial means will more than often be the losers. Especially hit will be migrant entrepreneurs whose cultures differ from ours in the West – where "Western democracy" is the only democracy that is valid.

Adding to the conversation as to who is ultimately benefiting from this endeavor from a cultural, social, geographical and ethnic perspective is the fact that "subconscious biases about race or gender, is a proven problem on many crowdsourced platforms."[19] Ultimately, this means that in order to acquire the needed support as a multimedia platform, the self-interest of the Western world must be at the fore with no concern for the Global South – other than what we can continue to steal from her. The inconvenient truth is that all roads lead to the same collective (if even subconscious) goal: the preservation of whiteness.

Rentzhog assures his audience that "our core, though, will remain, namely to empower our users to put pressure on world leaders so that they move faster towards an emission-free world and environmentally sustainable solutions and policies."[20]

An "emission-free world" sounds enticing – yet there are no plans whatsoever to retract our growth economies. "Environmentally sustainable solutions" ... according to who? According to a tribal elder who upholds the principles of "the seventh generation" (the Indigenous belief that humans must properly provide for its descendants by ensuring that our actions in the present allow the Earthly survival of seven succeeding generations – not to be confused with Unilever's Seventh Generation acquisition) – or according to the World Bank? (We all know the answer to this rhetorical question.)

Another inconvenient truth, regarding the above premise, is that there is growing pressure on governments to increase government research and development funding to develop and deploy "deep decarbonisation" technologies (NETS) as one of the primary "solutions" to climate change. At the 2015 United Nations Climate Change Conference (COP 21) in Paris, it was announced by Bill Gates, that 24 states would double their funding of "clean" energy research and development via the Mission Innovation initiative, founded and led by Gates (in partnership with these same states).

> *"We want it to cost more, in terms of revenue, public support and reputation, to not work on lowering emissions and improve environmental sustainability, whereas those that lead the way should be recognized for this. Our vision is to create a race towards environmental sustainability and CO2 neutrality, making it the core priority for businesses, politicians and organizations worldwide."*
> *— Acquisition International Magazine Issue 10, 2018*[21]

19 https://www.theverge.com/2015/10/28/9625968/rating-system-on-demand-economy-uber-olive-garden
20 Acquisition International Magazine Issue 10, 2018: https://www.acq-intl.com/issues/issue-10-2018/6/
21 Ibid.

Here again, we must look closely at language and framing. Who are "those that lead the way"? Are they referring to Western citizens who can fit all their belongings in a duffle bag? [Here it must be said that the environmental heroes in the West are NOT the Richard Bransons or Leonardo DiCaprios of the world. The real heroes for the environment, due to their almost non-existent environmental footprint, are the homeless – despite the scorn they receive from society as a whole.] Are they referring to the African Maasai who, to this day, literally leave no trace? Or are "those that lead the way" Unilever and Ikea (represented on the We Don't Have Time board)? This is another rhetorical question we all know the answer to. Notice the mention of CO2 "neutrality" rather than a drastic reduction of CO2 emissions. Convenient language when one of the main pillars of the business model is the sale of carbon offsets – rationalizing a continuance of the same carbon-based lifestyle by constructing a faux fantasy one, that anyone with monetary wealth, can buy into.

As online reviews and ratings systems have become a Western staple of determining the worthiness of a person, group or corporation, the Internet presently is a primary source of determining the quality of an entity. One example of this type of system is the online site Trip Advisor, which utilizes user feedback as a measuring stick of a hotel, airline, car rental, etc. As the Trip Advisor rating system is the revenue model We Don't Have Time seeks to emulate, we will explore this particular rating system.

Whereas a reputable and established website such as Trip Advisor is based on an actual experience – We Don't Have Time evaluations are more geared toward promises into the future regarding a green technology revolution and/or the effectiveness of advertising in making people believe the veracity of these promises. By utilizing fake accounts (think Twitter and Facebook), strategically orchestrated campaigns will effectively allow the app to break political careers and demonize people and countries based on the numbers of ratings ("climate bombs"). These bombs can be administered against any foe that does not embrace the technologies (sought by the West to benefit the West) of this so-called revolution, regardless if the reason for doing so is justifiable or not.

The word "bomb" itself will become reframed. Rather than associating bombs with militarism (never touched upon by We Don't Have Time) the word bomb will eventually become first and foremost associated with ratings, bad products, bad ideas and bad people. Such is the power of language and framing when combined with social engineering. Here, the behavioural economics of hatred can be weaponized – a virtual new form of soft power. The Nicaraguan Sandinista government who did not sign onto the Paris Agreement because it is too weak (and serves only Western interests) could quickly become a pariah on the global stage – as the West controls the stage. Already a target for destabilization, the soft power app would be applied as the ruling class sees fit.

When one contemplates the non-profit industrial complex, it must be considered the most powerful army in the world. Employing billions of staff, all interconnected, today's campaigns, financed by our ruling oligarchs can become viral in a matter of hours just by the interlocking directorate working together in unity toward a common goal to instill uniform thoughts and opinions, which gradually create a desired ideology. This is the art of social engineering. Conformity and emotive content as tools of manipulation has been and always will be the most powerful weapons in the Mad Men's toolbox. If 300,000 people have already voted with "climate hearts" on a "trending" topic in under 48 hours – it must be a great idea.

*"Nobody wants to be bottom of the class." — Ingmar Retzhog, We Don't Have Time, December 22, 2017, Nordic Business Insider*

To be clear, the West is in no position to "teach" (nudge/engineer) the "correct" value system regarding sustainability to the world, when the biggest polluters on the planet are manufactured into "climate leaders" and "climate heroes". This is reality turned on its head. A reality we are conditioned to accept. Institutions such as the United Nations in tandem with the media, spoon-feed this insanity (that defies all logic) to the global populace, in servitude to the ruling classes.

> important to foster that commitment and involve the staff in the strategic work. Post-launch, we will be dependent on a committed user base, and it will be very important to implement their feedback and nudge them towards being active on our platform. Our success hinges on building an active community around our core values."

"Nudging": Acquisition International Magazine Issue 10, 2018

Finally, this behavioural science platform lends itself to the continued devolvement of critical thinking. With virtually everything and everyone to rate all day long – who has time to look in depth at any given policy or product that after all, sounds, looks and feels simply amazing due to sophisticated marketing coupled with behavioural change tactics? It is vital to keep in mind that social engineering – and massive profit – are the key merits and purpose of this application.

# ACT II

## THE INCONVENIENT TRUTH BEHIND YOUTH CO-OPTATION

### WE DON'T HAVE TIME PLAYERS

**The We Don't Have Time board of directors comprises the following people:**

• Ingmar Rentzhog, We Don't Have Time founder and CEO

• Anette Nordvall,[22] We Don't Have Time chairwoman/shareholder, private tech investor, works with STOAF[23] (venture capital and private equity firm in Sweden), venture partner with Capital A Partners[24]

• David Olsson,[25] We Don't Have Time chief operating officer, chairman of the Swedish climate think tank Global Utmaning

• Christian Emmertz,[26] We Don't Have Time co-founder, business unit director at Hewlett Packard (HP) Sweden, partner at RealCap Investment,[27] The Climate Reality Project leader, trained by Al Gore

22 https://www.linkedin.com/in/anettenordvall/
23 http://www.stoaf.se/
24 http://www.capitalapartners.com/
25 https://www.linkedin.com/in/david-olsson-5b59983/
26 https://www.linkedin.com/in/christian-emmertz-41ab9415/
27 http://realcap.se/

• Stella Diesen,[28] "Changing the world with Microsoft tech Innofactor"[29] (formerly Microsoft), The Climate Reality Project leader, trained by Al Gore

• Gustav Stenbeck,[30] CEO of Mestro,[31] founder and executive chairman of Gain Sustain[32] (investment banking)

Global Utmaning, which translates to Global Challenge in English, was founded in 2005 by economist Kristina Persson,[33] Sweden's former Minister of Strategic Development and Nordic Cooperation. Persson was tasked with building co-operation with Nordic countries in order to leverage strength within the international community ("together we are an actor with clout"). Her position involved the fostering of long-term development for "the green transition, jobs and distribution, and initiatives to influence the global agenda for sustainable development."[34] She is heir (with her siblings) to the business empire[35] established by her father, Sven O. Persson, which has a revenue of approximately 3 billion USD (approx. $ 332,500,000.00) per annum. Persson is also the founder of the Freja Foundation[36] established in 2017.

**The We Don't Have Time Foundation board of directors includes:**

• Cathy Orlando, national director, Citizens Climate Lobby in Canada

• Stuart Scott, The Climate Reality Project leader, trained by Al Gore

• Per-Espen Stokenes, researcher in behavioural economics

• Ingmar Rentzhog, founder and CEO, We Don't Have Time

• David Olsson, chief operating officer, We Don't Have Time

• Greta Thunberg, special youth advisor and trustee

• Jamie Margolin, special youth advisor and trustee

28 https://www.linkedin.com/in/stelladiesen/
29 https://www.innofactor.com/
30 https://www.linkedin.com/in/gustavstenbeck/
31 http://mestro.se/
32 http://www.gainsustain.se/
33 https://www.globalutmaning.se/styrelse/kristina-persson/
34 https://sciblogs.co.nz/ariadne/2015/11/30/swedens-ministry-of-future-issues/
35 https://www.foretagskallan.se/foretagskallan-nyheter/lektionsmaterial/sven-o-persson/
36 http://www.frejafoundation.com/

"To ensure that our ambitious, value-driven agenda is not compromised, we have set up a 'good cause company', which means that the majority voting rights of the company belong to a charitable foundation. This foundation also owns the brand We Don't Have Time, and receives a revenue-based fee from the company. If our platform is successful, these revenues will be substantial, and the foundation can use these funds to support people and organizations that fight the climate crisis."

Acquisition International Magazine Issue 10, 2018

"Citizen Climate Lobby international outreach manager Cathy Orlando, centre, is pleased with the Trudeau government's new carbon tax plan. She's seen here with former U.S. Vice President Al Gore, husband Sanjiv Mathur, and their daughter Sophia Mathur."
37

37 https://www.sudbury.com/local-news/local-climate-activist-applauds-trudeau-governments-carbon-fee-plan-1098273

**The We Don't Have Time advisory board includes the following individuals:**

• Daniela Rogosic,[38] global press officer, the IKEA[39] Group

• Tove Ahlström,[40] CEO of Global Utmaning, affiliate of Al Gore's The Climate Reality Project

• Anna Svahn,[41] CEO of Feminvest,[42] CEO and co-founder at Cygnus Capital[43]

• Andra Farhad,[44] founder and CEO of Borshajen[45]

• Kaj Török,[46] chief reputation officer and chief sustainability officer of Max Burgers,[47] co-founder of Futerra Marketing and Advertising[48]

• Sweta Chakraborty,[49] renowned risk and behavioural scientist (behavioural change)[50]

• David JP Phillips,[51] founder of davidjpphillips.com, speakerrating.com and presentationsteknik.com. (Phillips delivers training in presentation skills in over 16 countries. His expertise is based on the latest research in neurology, psychology, and biology as a means of effective storytelling and communicating.)

WE MEAN BUSINESS NOW HERE

IKEA Foundation

---

38 https://www.linkedin.com/in/danielarogosic/
39 https://www.macleans.ca/economy/business/ikea-addresses-consumerism-in-the-age-of-peak-stuff/
40 https://en.globalutmaning.se/kansli/tove-ahlstrom/
41 https://www.linkedin.com/in/anna-svahn-52b02799/
42 http://www.feminvest.nu/?z=we-dont-have-time-har-fatt-globalt-momentum-7087
43 http://annasvahn.se/
44 https://www.linkedin.com/in/andra-farhad-39545210a/
45 https://borshajen.nu/om-borshajen/
46 https://www.linkedin.com/in/kajtorok/
47 https://www.maxburgers.com/
48 https://www.wearefuterra.com/
49 https://www.linkedin.com/in/swetachakraborty/
50 [Bio] http://swetachakraborty.com/
51 https://www.linkedin.com/in/davidjpphillips/

The presence of Ikea on the We Don't Have Time advisory board should be duly noted. In 2017, Ikea awarded a $44.6m grant[52] from the IKEA Foundation to the We Mean Business coalition (founded in 2014). This grant was in fact "the second largest single donation ever made by the charitable arm of retail giant IKEA." The We Mean Business coalition founding members include The B Team, the Business for Social Responsibility (BSR),[53] the Carbon Disclosure Project, Ceres, The Climate Group, the World Business Council for Sustainable Development (WBCSD), and the Prince of Wale's Corporate Climate Group. Other We Mean Business partners include the United Nations Global Compact, the United Nations Environment Programme (UNEP), UNEP Finance, the World Bank, and World Wildlife Fund.[54] [55]

The B Team is managed by Purpose, the for-profit public relations firm run by Avaaz co-founder Jeremy Heimans, co-author of the book "New Power". Ikea is a client of Purpose and partner to the Purpose NGO "We Are Here Now" ("Here Now").

In the following excerpt from the January 28, 2016, Maclean's article, *Have We Hit 'Peak Stuff?' Ikea Says There's Röom to Grow,*[56] the collective corporate climate fervor now sweeping the globe is demonstrated once again:

> *"So how to square Ikea's "peak stuff" talk with its "buy more" actions? A spokesperson volunteered in an email that [Steve] Howard's [head of sustainability at Ikea] comments were made as "part of a wider global context where many people still have very limited means" while Sjostrand suggested the goal was "to continue to grow our business, but grow it in a more sustainable way." Translation: Ikea will sell you more furniture and home furnishings, but it will try harder not to make you feel guilty about it. Which explains why the company's corporate reports are festooned with examples of sustainability initiatives, from selling only LED-compatible lighting to serving responsibly harvested fish in the cafeteria."*

Sustainability and capitalism are like oil and water. The two are incompatible. They cannot co-exist.

52 https://www.businessgreen.com/bg/news/3017979/ikea-foundation-beefs-up-we-mean-business-group-with-us-d446m-grant
53 https://www.bsr.org/en/membership/member-list
54 [Full list] https://www.wemeanbusinesscoalition.org/partners/
55 *[Further reading:"100 Billion for Everyone Who Signs"]* http://www.theartofannihilation.com/mckibbens-divest-ment-tour-brought-to-you-by-wall-street-part-xvii-of-an-investigative-report-100-billion-for-everyone-who-signs/
56 https://www.macleans.ca/economy/business/ikea-addresses-consumerism-in-the-age-of-peak-stuff/

The "climate revolution" sought by We Don't Have Time *et al* doesn't contract mass-consumption, it delivers new products in order to expand it.

The "clean energy revolution" doesn't threaten big oil – it secures it. It doesn't weaken capitalism. It strengthens it. It doesn't inspire resistance – it quells it – into oblivion.

Here we can reflect on the most simple things that shed light on the ideologies shared by the majority of those at the helm of decision making in addressing our climate crisis. In plain sight, what companies and institutions a person is most interested in are made public on one's LinkedIn account. Selected groups to follow shared by the average non-profit industrial complex (NPIC) professional, are rarely if ever groups, institutions or people working within the realms of ecology, Indigenous rights, social justice, environmental sciences, or other critical areas associated with climate change and environmental depletion. Nor are smaller institutions or individuals working toward small-scale local solutions of any interest.

Rather this interlocking directorate of "TED talkers" and "thought leaders" most commonly select and follow the world's most powerful and successful finance and tech companies, and the marketing firms that propel them to their success. The most popular institutions followed, and shared by most of this crowd, comprise white Western leadership, predominantly male. Some of the most admired ones chosen by the many are the World Economic Forum, the Bill and Melinda Gates Foundation, the United Nations Framework Convention on Climate Change (UNFCCC), the Economist, the Green Climate Fund – groups and institutions they wholly identify with, and seek to assimilate or belong to.

Here, we must recall the fact (disclosed in ACT I) that Al Gore's Climate Reality Project is a partner to We Don't Have Time. (Al Gore's priorities to be discussed in ACT III.)

> *"Rentzhog wants to affect change within business, not against business." — Anette Nordvall, Chairman of We Don't Have Time*[57]

57 https://nordic.businessinsider.com/this-swedish-crowdfunding-project-is-riffing-off-metoo-to-save-the-climate--/

## THE SACRIFICIAL LAMBS

> *"The same hormones and neurotransmitters can be released by a good story. These include dopamine, oxytocin, and endorphins, which Phillips refers to as the "angel's cocktail." The effects of oxytocin make you more generous, trusting, and ready to bond. This is what is released in your blood when you hear a sad story. It makes us feel relaxed and more human as we bond to the story-teller." — based on the TEDxStockholm Talk, "The Magical Science of Storytelling," by David JP Phillips, We Don't Have Time board of directors*[58]

To begin this segment, we can look at the "WE" movement ("ME to WE", Free the Children and WE Day).[59] The 2015 exposé "Unleashing Voluntourism"[60] produced by the Canadian Public Broadcasting (CBC) was originally scheduled to air on March 19, 2015. The documentary investigated the privatization of, the NGOization of, and the explosive growth of, what has morphed into a billion dollar industry – tourism masquerading as volunteerism – for privileged youth in the West.

Celebrity, fetishized in a rapidly eroding society void of meaning and culture, has resulted in such a powerful asset to capitalism and militarism that the subject has become an active area of study by academics such as Dan Brockington[61] and Ilan Kapoor.[62] The power of celebrity was not lost on WE, whose keynote speakers for massive gatherings and endorsements have included: Canadian Prime Minister Justin Trudeau in 2008,[63] and again in 2015, following Obama's election win, former "first lady" Michelle Obama, Hollywood's Natalie Portman and a stream of others.[64] Indeed, renting celebrities for galas and events has too become a niche industry.

Shortly before it was to air, the documentary was pulled[65] after WE requested unauthorized footage be removed from the exposé. When it did air, on April 7,

---

58 https://www.thecoachingroom.com.au/blog/the-powerful-effects-of-functional-storytelling

59 "According to WE.org, 'WE is made up of WE Charity and ME to WE. Both are part of the WE Movement, also known as 'WE' and 'We.'" – "WE Charity used to be called Free The Children, and before that, Kids Can Free The Children. ME to WE is a private, for-profit business, but WE prefers to call it a 'social enterprise.'" [Source: https://www.canadalandshow.com/craig-kielburger-founded-we-to-fight-child-labour-now-the-we-brand-promotes-products-made-by-children/]

60 https://www.cbc.ca/doczone/episodes/volunteers-unleashed

61 https://celebrityanddevelopment.wordpress.com/about-dan-brockington/

62 https://www.academia.edu/19789544/Celebrity_Humanitarianism_the_Ideology_of_Global_Charity_Routledge_2013_

63 https://youtu.be/Jl58_gJwP9s

64 https://www.we.org/we-day/what-is-we-day/celebrity-ambassadors/

65 https://www.canadalandshow.com/why-did-cbc-just-pull-expose-voluntourism/

2017, two scenes had been cut from the film. The clip *"Volunteers Unleashed: suppressed Me to We clip #1"*[66] is one of the two deleted clips.

The controversy regarding WE is far from over as the NGO grapples to protect its million dollar brand.[67] On January 17, 2019, WE announced they would commence legal action against a small podcast network and news outlet[68] in Manitoba, Canada, where journalists have no explicit legal protection from SLAPP lawsuits (Strategic Lawsuits Against Public Participation). This news outlet had been reporting on the WE movement[69] since 2015.

The following images and brief commentaries are but a tiny glimpse into the world of NGOization and co-optation of both resistance and youth. Today we bear witness to what can aptly be described as the mechanisms and orchestrated movements of the non-profit industrial spectacle.

To illustrate the co-optation of youth, we will now look at the celebrity youth activists, and Climate Reality leaders Greta Thunberg and Jamie Margolin. We focus on these two individuals, as they are directly connected to the We Don't Have Time campaign and business plan.

The Climate Reality Project and Global Utmaning. Greta Thunberg at far left. "How do we ensure that today's decision-makers benefit and learn from young people's commitment to the future? On September 26, the question attracted over 250 visitors to Kulturhuset Stadsteatern where Global Utmaning and Al Gore's Climate Reality Project arranged seminars."
70

66 https://youtu.be/Qzl4xDVjyvc
67 https://twitter.com/CharlieAngusNDP/status/1086019462728318976
68 https://twitter.com/CANADALAND/status/1085914595007574017/photo/1
69 https://www.canadalandshow.com/podcast/the-canadaland-investigation-of-the-kielburgers-we-movement/
70 https://www.globalutmaning.se/vem-bryr-sig-om-framtiden/

Thunberg has stated repeatedly that her strike will continue "until Sweden is aligned with the Paris Agreement." Therefore, by her own statements, this is the singular, overall purpose and goal of the strike. The foundation of the Paris Agreement is the expansion of nuclear, the financialization of nature, further privatization at an unprecedented scale, "large scale CO2 reduction" (carbon capture and storage), a desperate attempt to revitalize economic growth, and more market "solutions" that will further perpetuate our multiple crises. Therefore, the Thunberg campaign is in part to create a demand upon governments across the globe to align with the Paris Agreement. (A demand to obtain what the ruling classes have already decided to unleash on us, our planet, and all life.) As adherence to the Paris Accords is a running theme within the mainstream NGO movement, the marketing campaign is helped along by 350.org, Avaaz, WWF, Greenpeace, in tandem with the UN ("Changing Together"), the World Bank ("Stepping Up")[71] and, more recently, the World Economic Forum (WEF).

71 The COP24 *Stepping Up Climate Action* is a campaign initiated by the UN with Connect4Climate. The campaign of "global leaders, thinkers, activists and influencers" includes Greta Thunberg. "Connect4Climate is a global partnership program under the Communication for Climate Change Multi-Donor Trust Fund of the World Bank Group. The Trust Fund was initiated by the Italian Ministry of Environment, and in 2014 it was joined by the German Federal Ministry for Economic Cooperation and Development."
https://youtu.be/9LaSEEEK37A

The Global Utmaning think tank cites as its main asset its network of over 90 senior advisors.[72] From its homepage:

> *"The global market economy has lifted millions of people out of poverty. Meanwhile, inequality increased significantly. The financial system must be globally regulated and* ***the current economic stagnation broken****. It requires a new green, circular and inclusive growth model that creates value, labor and welfare. What is tomorrow's new economic story?"*

Global Utmaning recently announced[73] a partnership with Global Shapers – an initiative of the World Economic Forum bringing together young leaders worldwide: "The World Economic Forum Annual Meeting 2019 will be held on January 22-25 in Davos-Klosters, Switzerland. Over 3,000 global leaders will come together under the theme Globalization 4.0: **Shaping a Global Architecture in the Age of the Fourth Industrial Revolution**." *[Emphasis added]*

72 http://www.globalutmaning.se/radgivare/alla-seniora-radgivare/

73 https://www.globalutmaning.se/tankesmedjan-global-utmaning-och-global-shapers-stockholm-inleder-samarbete/

## AVAAZ

Here we will make some brief observations of both Avaaz and 350.org in relation to the global "Climate Strike" campaigns. An exhaustive body of research that lays bare the function and ancestry of both NGOs, based on investigations from 2012 to the present, now exists on the Wrong Kind of Green website.[74] I encourage readers to familiarize themselves with the two entities.

On December 14, 2018, 350.org sent out a press release[75] containing the following excerpts:

> *"Katowice, Poland – Today- 30 school children from three local schools in Katowice, answered the call of Greta Thunberg and brought the global #ClimateStrike into the final day of the UN Climate talks in Katowice.*
>
> *The 30 students were granted special access to enter the UN talks and carry their message to the delegates and Polish government: with only 12 years left to get the world off fossil fuels, leaders must act now." [emphasis in original]*

On cue, the international media[76] would publish photos such as this one:

74 http://www.wrongkindofgreen.org/
75 https://350.org/press-release/polish-school-children-join-call-for-global-climate-strike-at-un-climate-talks-in-katowice/
76 https://www.bbc.co.uk/programmes/w172w25jl5nvpnz

Here is what you don't see:

Preconference: The youth are being organized for the December 14, 2018 press event. Photo: David Tong / WWF New Zealand

Directions are given. Listen up kids. Photo: David Tong / WWF New Zealand

And here, we see a media frenzy, clamouring to get the attention of a single man. The youth stand silent, ignored in the background. Yet the youth were supposed to have been exactly what the action was about. "Adults sometimes forget about the young people," said Magorzata Czachowska, one of the Polish students inspired by Thunberg. Photo: David Tong / WWF New Zealand

Here we have youth - bored out of their minds. Is this activism? Is this what revolution looks like? Photo: David Tong / WWF New Zealand

Hello Iain Keith. Iain Keith - campaign director for Avaaz. Photo: David Tong / WWF New Zealand

The bored youth are successfully herded and put into place - ready for the photo-op. Photo: David Tong / WWF New Zealand

At the bottom of the 350.org press release under the heading "For more information", the press release discloses: *"NOTE that 350.Org and Avaaz are NOT organising these actions but are helping the students to spread their message." [Emphasis in original]*

And yet, it certainly appears that Avaaz did in fact play a leading role in organsizing the action – while orchestrating the media spotlight. [See photos on the previous page.]

On the day following the 350.org-Avaaz press release, December 15, 2018, NGOs and institutions alike scrambled to catapult the words of Thunberg into the hearts and minds of citizens all over the world. From the UN, to Avaaz, to the World Bank, to grass-roots resistance, they all clamoured to spread young Thunberg's words. But one NGO took it upon itself to redact many of Thunberg's words, releasing an abbreviated version[77] (79K views on Facebook). With no disclaimer to its audience, Avaaz removed four excerpts from Thunberg's speech.[78]

77 https://www.facebook.com/Avaaz/videos/326051374664351/

78 1) "You only speak of the green eternal economic growth because you are too scared of being unpopular. You only talk about moving forward with the same bad ideas that got us into this mess even when the only sensible thing to do is pull the emergency brake."
2) "But I don't care about being popular. I care about climate justice and the living planet our civilisation is being sacrificed for the opportunity of a very small number of people to continue making enormous amounts of money."
3) "Until you start focusing on what needs to be done rather than what is politically possible, there is no hope. We cannot solve a crisis without treating it as a crisis."
4) "We have run out of excuses and we are running out of time."

The two excerpts that follow, which were cut by Avaaz, are most revealing:

> *"You only speak of the green eternal economic growth because you are too scared of being unpopular. You only talk about moving forward with the same bad ideas that got us into this mess, even when the only sensible thing to do is pull the emergency brake."*
>
> *"But I don't care about being popular. I care about climate justice and the living planet. Our civilisation is being sacrificed for the opportunity of a very small number of people to continue making enormous amounts of money."*

It is not surprising Avaaz would strike Greta's comments considering that a primary function of Avaaz is to promote market solutions which accelerate "green" economic growth – in servitude to "a very small number of people to continue making enormous amounts of money."

In the following Avaaz campaign, the NGO employs Thunberg's face to place pressure on Sweden for corporate non-solutions, such as in this instance, "large scale CO2 reduction". This is holistic framing for carbon capture and storage technologies.

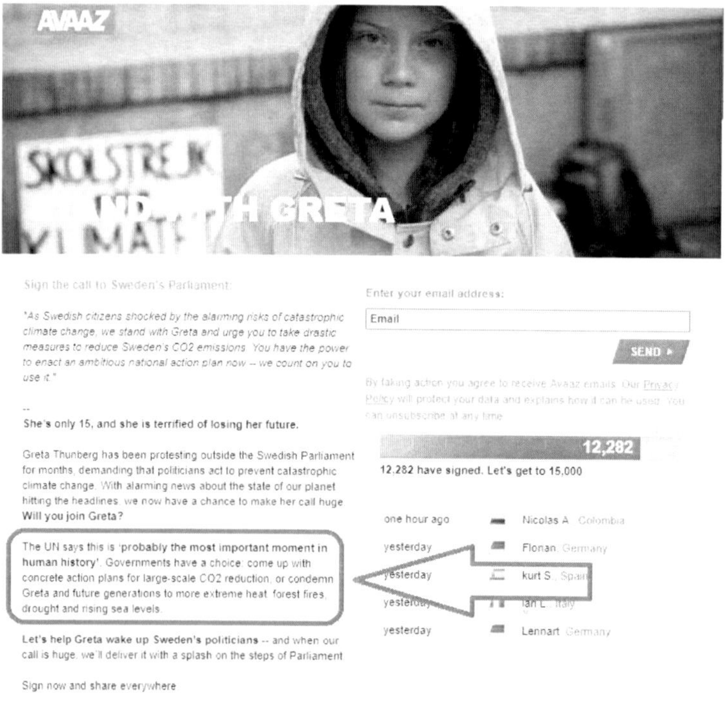

Here it is imperative to refer to the August 24, 2017 press release[79] "Bellona seminar on Nordic CCS cooperation". From the release:

> *"Now politicians have to go ahead so that we can build full-scale CO2 capture facilities as quickly as possible,' said Tandberg. Three full-scale facilities in Norway are planned, but not yet granted, with a preliminary price tag of NOK 12.6 billion (EUR 1.28 billion)...*
>
> *Norway is leading in capture, transportation and storage technologies, and can export the knowledge and facilities. There is potential for a completely new industry to be built. However it depends on whether Norway is able to keep its position. It is urgent to build the CCS plants, develop the technology further and get full-scale CCS infrastructure, and a Nordic cooperation can facilitate this process."*

This is a prime example of one of the main functions of NGOs. To generate popular demand from the citizenry who will in turn support the legislation required for projects that serve to benefit industry, rather than people and planet. Prior to the contracts being signed or a shovel breaking ground to build the infrastructures that will comprise the "global architecture in the age of the fourth industrial revolution" – legislation is required. And just like a proverbial snowball turning into an avalanche, the legislation begets money for a budget with bidding and construction to commence shortly thereafter.

What better way to create a demand for something detrimental to both the environment and the populace, than to package it under climate change solutions, with the lovely and innocent face of Greta. With reality turned on its head, industry doesn't have to impose its will on the people – the people will impose it on themselves, via Avaaz *et al.* The people are thus engineered to demand the very false solutions that the corporations have had up their sleeves for years, and even decades.

Hence, the non-profit industrial complex and the media, both financed by the world's power elite, are amalgamated with and by corporate power. Together they work in unity, toward one common goal: economic growth. Hence, market solutions are always THE solutions. It is not simply a matter of placing the economy first before everything else. Rather, it is placing the economy first at the EXPENSE of everything else. And everyone else. And all life on this planet.

79 http://bellona.org/news/ccs/2017-12-24303

To look at the scale of such so-called solutions, one need look no further than the 2013 Carbon Tracker "Unburnable Carbon Report"[80] – page 12:

> *"Given that the average annual rate of storage in 2015 is projected by the Global Carbon Capture and Storage Institute (2012) to be about 2.25 million tonnes for 16 CCS projects,* ***a total of nearly 3800 CCS projects would need to be operating by 2050*** *under the idealised scenario."*

The idealized scenario "offers about an 80% chance of not exceeding a warming of more than 2°C."

May 14, 2015:

> *"As with all the shaping of our shared futures by the elite, the pathway to CCS is clear in the 2008 Green Alliance paper, A Last Chance for Coal, with contributions from Ben Caldecott while at the Policy Exchange think tank. The paper notes that it is critical Europe's commitment to CCS be realized before 2020; 12 short years away from the paper's publication date.* ***The year 2020 is a critical date of vast significance – a recurring deadline for all environmental market solutions to be in place."***

*[Further reading: AVAAZ: The Globe's Largest & Most Powerful Behavioural Change Network]*[81]

*[Further reading: McKibben's Divestment Tour – Brought to You by Wall Street]*[82]

80 http://www.carbontracker.org/wp-content/uploads/2014/09/Unburnable-Carbon-2-Web-Version.pdf
81 http://www.wrongkindofgreen.org/2017/07/27/avaaz-the-globes-largest-most-powerful-behavioural-change-network-part-i/
82 http://www.wrongkindofgreen.org/2013/05/17/mckibbens-divestment-tour-brought-to-you-by-wall-street/

# JAMIE MARGOLIN – ZERO HOUR

"Donate": Jamie Margolin, teenage founder of This Is Zero Hour | Climate Reality Project webpage banner

Jamie Margolin is the teenage founder of This Is Zero Hour[83] and "one of the 13 plaintiffs suing Washington State[84] for its failure to take adequate action on climate change." (As disclosed in ACT I of this series, Margolin – and her NGO Zero Hour – accounted for two of the six accounts tagged by We Don't Have Time on the very first post reporting Greta Thunberg's school strike). Margolin attended Al Gore's Climate Reality Leadership Corps (a three-day conference) that took place in Seattle on June 27-29, 2017.[85] In July 2017, Margolin began organizing for a youth climate march in Washington, D.C. and launched Zero Hour. On February 27, 2018, exactly eight months after her first day at the Climate Reality Leadership Corps, Margolin would be featured in Rolling Stone magazine. Prior to her meteoric rise to stardom, Margolin interned in Hillary Clinton's campaign office in Seattle. The following passage demonstrates what has now become the normal corporate promotion of youth:

> *"The youngest speaker at the Global Climate Action Summit in San Francisco this week is Jamie Margolin[86] of Seattle, who founded the Zero Hour youth climate march[87] this past July and led its flagship action in Washington, D.C. At 16, Margolin presents a youthful contrast to most of the GCAS leadership, like California Governor Jerry Brown (80); former New York City Mayor Michael Bloomberg (76); and China's top climate diplomat, Xie Zhenhua (68)."* [88]

83 http://thisiszerohour.org/
84 https://www.ourchildrenstrust.org/washington/
85 https://www.greenpeace.org/usa/stories/faces-of-the-future/
86 https://psmag.com/environment/zero-hour-inside-the-youth-climate-march
87 http://thisiszerohour.org/the-march/
88 https://psmag.com/environment/at-the-gcas-in-san-francisco-the-youth-have-a-voice

In the 21st century manufactured movements and revolutions, today's "leaders" (fabricated by corporate owned and funded media) are no longer enemies of the establishment. Rather, they do events together – with establishment figures such as New York City Mayor, Bill de Blasio adulating over[89] our new "revolutionaries" while tagging them and tweeting their praises. When the establishment itself loves our movements and our "faces of the future"[90] – we know we have already lost tomorrow.

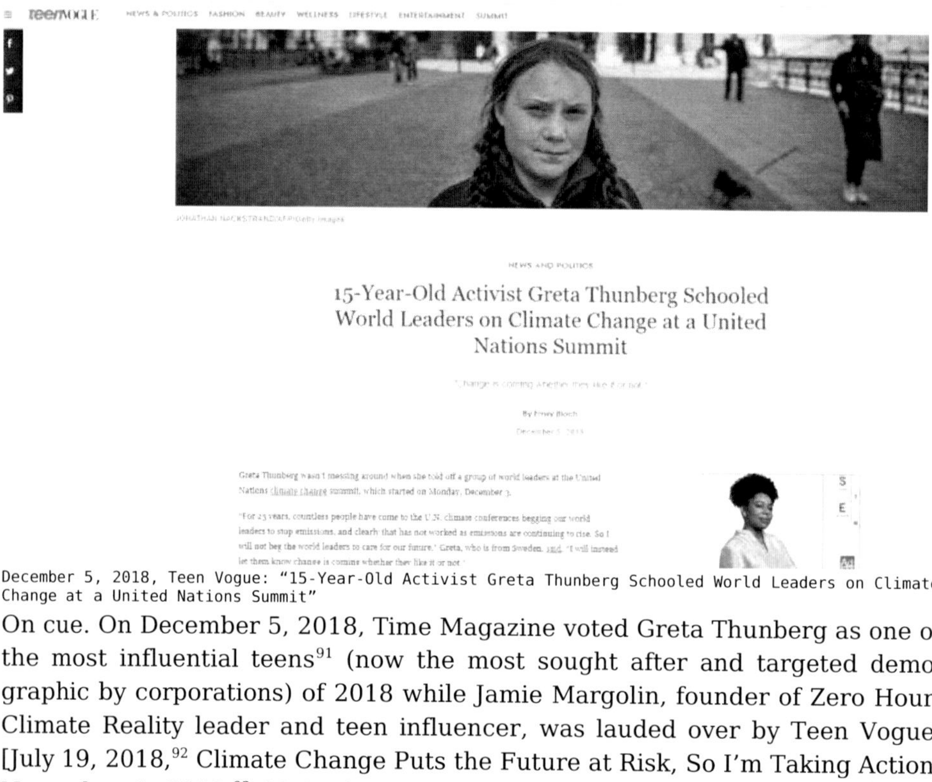

NEWS AND POLITICS

15-Year-Old Activist Greta Thunberg Schooled World Leaders on Climate Change at a United Nations Summit

Greta Thunberg wasn't messing around when she told off a group of world leaders at the United Nations climate change summit, which started on Monday, December 3.

"For 25 years, countless people have come to the U.N. climate conferences begging our world leaders to stop emissions, and clearly that has not worked as emissions are continuing to rise. So I will not beg the world leaders to care for our future," Greta, who is from Sweden, said. "I will instead let them know change is coming whether they like it or not."

December 5, 2018, Teen Vogue: "15-Year-Old Activist Greta Thunberg Schooled World Leaders on Climate Change at a United Nations Summit"

On cue. On December 5, 2018, Time Magazine voted Greta Thunberg as one of the most influential teens[91] (now the most sought after and targeted demographic by corporations) of 2018 while Jamie Margolin, founder of Zero Hour, Climate Reality leader and teen influencer, was lauded over by Teen Vogue. [July 19, 2018,[92] Climate Change Puts the Future at Risk, So I'm Taking Action; November 5, 2018,[93] 21 Under 21: Jamie Margolin Knows Climate Justice is the Key to All Justice; December 1, 2018,[94] The Teen Vogue Summit 2018]

89 https://www.facebook.com/NYCMayor/videos/jamie-margolin-zero-hour/2104186793180766/
90 https://www.greenpeace.org/usa/stories/faces-of-the-future/
91 http://time.com/5463721/most-influential-teens-2018/
92 https://www.teenvogue.com/story/climate-change-puts-the-future-at-risk-so-im-taking-action
93 https://www.teenvogue.com/story/jamie-margolin-21-under-21-2018
94 https://www.teenvogue.com/gallery/teen-vogue-summit-2018-photo-booth

In the image below, Margolin lends her celebrity status to prop up the brands Global Citizen and Johnson & Johnson. Global Citizen is perhaps the most egregious NGO in the non-profit industrial complex with its grotesque model of shallow, hollowed-out "activism" and corporatization. Recently Global Citizen has introduced "points" that can be accumulated by clicking on actions. In a blatant emulation of credit cards (the more money you spend, the more points you acquire), the more actions you click, the more points you acquire.

These points can then be redeemed for access to celebrity events and concerts.

This is the social engineering of unquestioning compliance and instantaneous acquiescence. In order to receive the reward, one must perform the action requested. If you do not comply, you simply do not receive the points. Here, the encouragement for critical thought and debate is deliberately and strategically erased from the equation.

September 25, 2018: The Zero Hour Movement founder & Executive Director Jamie Margolin attends Global Citizen – Movement Makers at The Times Center. in New York City.(Photo by Noam Galai/Getty Images for Global Citizen)

NGOs are not the only entities to exploit youth. Corporate partners that finance their endeavours also provide lofty sums of money to have their toxic legacies greenwashed. In July 2018, Johnson & Johnson was ordered to pay "nearly $4.7 billion US in total damages to 22 women and their families after they claimed asbestos in Johnson & Johnson talcum powder contributed to their ovarian cancer, in the first case against the company that focused on asbestos in the powder... Six of the 22 plaintiffs in the latest trial have died from ovarian cancer. ... Mark Lanier, lead counsel for the plaintiffs, said in a statement that Johnson & Johnson had covered up evidence of asbestos in their products for more than 40 years."[95]

Par for the course, partnerships and endorsements for corporations inflicting violence upon both children and planet are a hallmark of the non-profit industrial complex. This is not the only lawsuit that has been launched against Johnson & Johnson nor will it be the last. There are also 1,200 pending lawsuits[96] in the US alone against this corporate entity. Johnson & Johnson is not the exception – it is the norm.

"Global Citizen – Movement Makers. In This Photo (L-R): Ladan Manteghi, Jamie Margolin, and Afroz Shah speak onstage during Global Citizen – Movement Makers at The Times Center on September 25, 2018 in New York City." Source: Noam Galai/Getty Images North America

95 https://www.cbc.ca/news/world/johnson-johnson-talc-powder-cancer-lawsuit-1.4745406
96 https://www.rochongenova.com/Current-Class-Action-Cases/Talc-Powder-class-action.shtml

Bill Gates (Breakthrough Energy, Mission Innovation) with Canadian Prime Minister Justin Trudeau for Global Citizen. Montreal, Quebec, Canada, September 17, 2016. REUTERS/Geoff

= TIME TIME's 25 Most Influential Teens o...

**Greta Thunberg, 15**

Getty Images (2)

Before Sweden's general elections in September, Thunberg went on a three-week strike from school in an effort to urge her government to act on climate change. "I thought that nothing is happening and no one is doing anything – it is my moral duty to do what I can," she tells TIME of her mission. "I cannot vote, so this is a way that I can make my voice heard." Since then, Thunberg has inspired hundreds of similar school strikes around the world, including a mass school walkout in Australia. She has also been nominated for an international prize for her activism and recently met with the U.N. Secretary General at the COP24 climate summit in Poland. She plans to strike every Friday until Sweden is aligned with the Paris Agreement on climate change; while the Scandinavian country is one of only a handful in Europe actively pursuing policies to meet the climate goals, Thunberg says it is not enough. In October, she took her message to a crowd of more than 10,000 at a climate change demonstration in Helsinki. "Instead of worrying about the future, you should try to change it while you still can." –*Suvin Haynes*

June 30, 2017, Twitter: Jamie Margolin – teenage founder and executive director of This Is Zero Hour, founded in 2017

Jamie Margolin, speaking via Skype at the Climate Emergency Plan presentation (We Don't Have Time, Global Utmaning, the Club of Rome), November 24, 2018:[97]

> *"We don't just think about, oh there's carbon in the air and we need to lower it, we think of how did the carbon get there?, like how did we allow a system that could lead us to such destruction?"*

The system that Margolin refers to is that of global capitalism, an economic system that is devouring everything in its path. A promise to destroy the planetary ecosystems of our shared futures. And it is not as though Margolin has not begun to understand the glaring systems intersecting at the nexus of our multiple crises, such as capitalism, colonialism, racism and patriarchy.

September 26, 2018, Twitter: Jamie Margolin, Global Citizen ["If voting changed anything, they'd make it illegal." - Emma Goldman]

Rather, Margolin does in fact possess the basic building blocks of knowledge required for the long road ahead of instilling and inspiring the revolutionary changes that are required amongst the youth. Yet by positioning herself with those that bring into fruition and profit from everything Margolin touches upon, she tragically denigrates her own analysis by merely calling for better cups for Starbucks[98] rather than the elimination of Starbucks altogether. Hence, on her current path, Margolin does more harm than good for the very systemic issues she articulates so well.

97 https://youtu.be/7vwdF10MIVg
98 https://youtu.be/s-8xAs5XWvY

EXPLORE People

Jamie Margolin (left) and Nadia Nazar

November 2, 2018, People Magazine: This Is Zero Hour, Youth Climate March

teenVOGUE NEWS & POLITICS FASHION BEAUTY WELLNESS LIFESTYLE ENTERTAINMENT SUM

Photo: Drew Escriva

27/31

21 Under 21 honoree Jamie Margolin turned the summit into the ultimate networking opportunity — the sign of a true changemaker.

Send Us a Tip

RollingStone

HOME > CULTURE > CULTURE FEATURES

FEBRUARY 27, 2018 5:57PM ET

# Meet the Teens Schooling Us on Climate Action

**Zero Hour, a national movement mobilizing youth to protect a livable future, is planning a youth march this summer**

*By* ERIC HOLTHAUS

February 27, 2017, Rolling Stone: Jamie Margolin - Youth Founder of This Is Zero Hour

**The Climate Group**

Zero Hour NYC, a student-led coalition, will march in DC on July 21st for environmental justice, with sister marches taking place all over the world. How will you lend your voice to the story? @ThisIsZeroHour bit.ly/ZeroHourMarch

THIS IS ZERO HOUR

9 Retweets 14 Likes

July 17, 2018, Twitter: The Climate Group, This Is Zero Hour

**Al Gore** @algore

So inspired by these young leaders taking to the streets this Saturday for #ThisIsZeroHour. Make your voices heard in our fight to solve the climate crisis!

> 3 DAYS THIS IS ZERO HOUR JULY 21ST
>
> **Zero Hour** @ThisIsZeroHour
>
> Only THREE DAY to go! We're busy preparing for the historic youth climate march on July 21st. Tomorrow, we lobby. Friday, we build. Saturday, we march.

2:10 PM - 18 Jul 2018

321 Retweets 955 Likes

51 321 955

July 18, 2018, Twitter: Al Gore, Generation Investment, This Is Zero Hour

**Mayor Bill de Blasio** @NYCMayor

Our young people are leading the fight for change. This weekend, they'll march in our city and around the globe because the future of our planet — their future — is at stake. #ThisIsZeroHour

1:49 PM - 18 Jul 2018

95 Retweets 177 Likes

26 95 177

July 18, 2018, Twitter: NYC Mayor Bill De Blasio, This Is Zero Hour

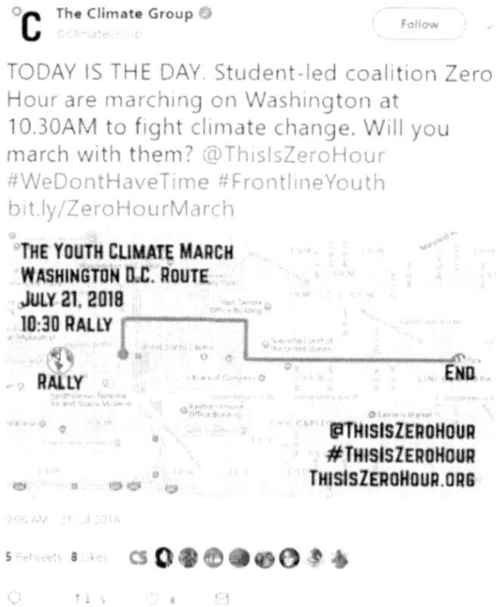


July 21, 2018, Twitter: The Climate Group, This Is Zero Hour, We Don't Have Time, Frontline Youth

July 23, 2018, Twitter: Climate Nexus, This Is Zero Hour

September 15, 2018, Twitter: NYC Mayor Bill De Blasio with Jamie Margolin, Youth Founder of This Is Zero Hour

September 19, 2018, Instagram: NYC Mayor Bill De Blasio, This Is Zero Hour

The Black Panthers (1966) with the raised-fist salute - a symbol of black power and the human rights movement at large

September 20, 2018: Al Gore, The Climate Reality Project with Jamie Margolin, Youth Founder of This Is Zero Hour

The Black Panthers (1966) with the raised-fist salute - a symbol of black power and the human rights movement at large

With "crude capitalists"[99], such as Gore, de Blasio and others, now capturing the last vestiges of youth that even have such awareness (an awareness that is slowly dying out), soon the systemic structures allowing capitalism and oppression to flourish will have no opposition whatsoever. We are reaching the point where there is no distinction between our "movements" and the coalitions created to further our oppression and servitude. The fact that Margolin serves as a face for Al Gore's Climate Reality Project – when saving capitalism is Gore's number one priority (as we will learn in ACT III), grinds all of Margolin's articulate words – and actions – to dust. Gore uses Greta, Margolin and all the youth they mobilize – by destroying the very futures these youth are hoping to save – all in servitude to economic growth and capitalism for the world's power elite.

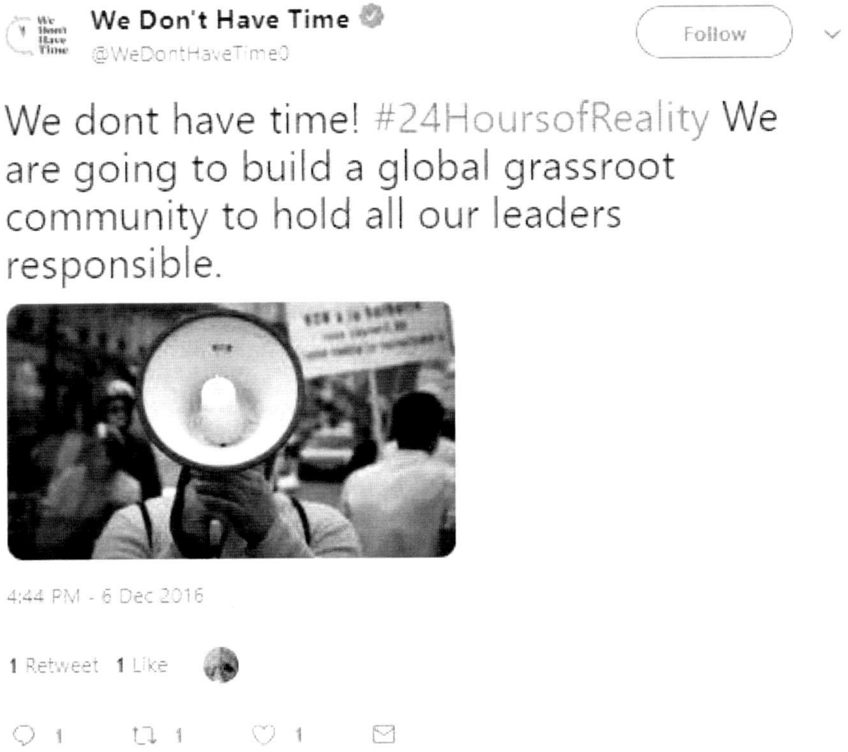


99 https://youtu.be/wDxeaizRRAs

Also of relevance to the Thunberg campaign is the race to capture the Millennial and Generation Z. With increasing frequency, this capture is primarily achieved by the manufactured and heavily funded youth "movements". "Movements" teeming with potential consumers, fully exploitable by those that benefit from, and in many cases contribute to, the steady stream of funding. The title Generation Z has been applied to those connected from birth to online media, to whom "instant gratification is the norm." Today, this demographic is the most powerful and sought after audience in North America. As an illustration of the term's popularity, Zero Hour's Margolin actually refers to herself[100] as "Generation Z."

The November 8, 2018 Barclays article, *Gen Z: Step Aside Millennials*[101] reports that this demographic (children born between 1995 and 2009), the same demographic that youth leaders like Greta Thunberg and Jamie Margolin, belong to, appeal to and influence, are quickly becoming the new "consumer giants" and "mega influencers":

> *"By 2020, Generation Z will be the largest group of consumers globally. They will account for 40% of consumers in the US, Europe and BRIC countries and 10% in the rest of the world. Companies that don't engage with Gen Z successfully could rapidly lose market share. Some of them may only be 9 years old, but Gen Z already have huge spending power. In the US, Gen Z currently have $200 billion in direct buying power but $1 trillion in indirect spending power by influencing household spending*. Gen Z's advanced digital knowledge and ability to assess factors such as price and availability from a young age make them increasingly influential in family spending decisions."*

In the eyes of bankers and capitalists, this group of youth are mere consumers. Dollar signs. Not children, youth, or even people.

Faux activism comes with many perks inclusive of six-figure salaries, jet-setting, and "TED Talks". Plus, the best hipster eco-brands money can buy. Perhaps the most enticing perk – is access. Access to the halls of power. With the media fawning all over every reformist word, the faux activist can fall in love with his/her/x own image all over again. Everyone wants to be a star. Everyone wants to live the luxurious life. Everyone wants to belong to the champagne circuit.

100 https://psmag.com/environment/at-the-gcas-in-san-francisco-the-youth-have-a-voice
101 https://www.investmentbank.barclays.com/our-insights/generation-z.html

All on the backs of the most oppressed. All on the backs of the most vulnerable. Yet the paradox is this – we are their vehicle. Our resistance captured and channeled directly back into the very systems crushing us.

## A COUP DE GRACE

Greta Thunberg is being strategically exploited by the World Bank, the UN, and the non-profit industrial complex that serves the ruling classes. They are using her to advance their own self-interests and objectives – that are in direct opposition to everything this young woman brilliantly articulates. This is being presented as a "leaderless movement" – very much the "New Power" methodology and religion for the capitalists – theorized by Jeremy Heimans (Avaaz/Purpose) for mass movement building – that serves the most powerful and destructive forces on the planet.

The manipulation of young, malleable minds is at the foundation of Western indoctrination in order to insulate a failing system and mask the market solutions being designed to address it. Market "solutions" that benefit the rich at the expense of the environment. Hence, the youth are always the sacrificial lambs of the non-profit industrial complex.[102]

102 *[Further reading: From Stable to Star – The Making of North American "Climate Heroes":* http://www.theartofannihilation.com/from-stable-to-star-the-making-of-north-american-climate-heroes/]
*[Further Reading: Targeting Millennials: The 30 Trillion Dollar Jackpot:* http://www.theartofannihilation.com/mckibbens-divestment-tour-brought-to-you-by-wall-street-part-x-targeting-millennials-the-30-trillion-dollar-jackpot/]
*[Further Reading: The Pygmalion Virus in Three Acts [2017 AVAAZ SERIES, PART II:* http://www.theartofannihilation.com/the-pygmalion-virus-in-three-acts-2017-avaaz-series-part-ii/]

# ACT III

## THE MOST INCONVENIENT TRUTH: "CAPITALISM IS IN DANGER OF FALLING APART"

### MALENA ERNMAN: WWF ENVIRONMENTAL HERO OF THE YEAR, 2017

Greta Thunberg's mother and father. Opera singer Malena Ernman with husband actor Svante Thunberg at the Polar Music Prize 2012. Ernman represented Sweden in the Eurovision Song Contest in 2009. Photo: Chapman

In October 2018, Miljö & Utveckling recognized We Don't Have Time founder, Ingmar Rentzhog, as Sweden's number 1 Environmental Influencer of the Year.[103]

Greta Thunberg, special youth advisor and trustee to the foundation established by the burgeoning mainstream tech start-up We Don't Have Time, was recognized as the number 2 Influencer of the Year.

tps://miljo-utveckling.se/ingmar-rentzhog-ar-arets-miljoinfluencer-2018/

Top 4 List of Environmental Impacts of the Year 2018

**1. Ingmar Rentzhog.** He is chairman of Global Challenge and CEO and founder of the company and the network We Don't Have Time. He has a background in financial communication and has devoted his time to fighting climate change.
**Twitter account: @ WeDontHaveTime0**

**2. Greta Thunberg.** 15-year-old Greta climbed outside Sweden's parliament for 15 days, which has been rewritten in international media. She is the daughter of the opera singer and climate debater Malena Ernman.
**Twitter account: @GretaThunberg**

103 [Source: The Secret Sauce of a Global Climate Movement https://medium.com/wedonthavetime/the-secret-sauce-of-a-global-climate-movement-6336f01da2d]

The previous month, on September 1, 2018,[104] Dagens Nyheter, Sweden's most prominent newspaper, ran an op-ed from Global Challenge titled "The Acute Climate Crisis Requires a Broad Political Gathering":

"Although much of the change required is both possible and profitable, vigorous political campaigns are essential to adjust prices, taxes and regulations so that the transition to a sustainable society becomes attractive, profitable and fast."[105]

"The signatories stand ready to assist in the process, in support of transforming our society and the wider world into a low-carbon economy: Mats Andersson, Vice Chairman of the Global Challenges Foundation; Erik Brandsma, CEO of Jämtkraft; **Malena Ernman, Opera Singer**; Antje Jackelén, Archbishop; Staffan Laestadius, Professor Emeritus KTH; Kristina Persson, former Minister of the Future; **Ingmar Rentzhog, Chairman of the Global Development Challenge**; Johan Rockström, Professor of Environmental Sciences SU; Daniel Sachs, CEO of Proventus; and Anders Wijkman, Chairman of the Club of Rome."

Anders Wijkman, cited in the above signatories, is a former member of parliament, chairman of the Swedish Environment Council and former co-president of the Club of Rome. He is also a member of Global Utmaning[106] with a special commitment to climate issues and circular finances.

Also cited among the signatories is Malena Ernman, mother of Greta Thunberg.

In an interview published on October 15, 2018,[107] recognizing Rentzhog as the "#1 Environmental Influencer of the Year", Miljö & Utveckling asks Rentzhog who are his greatest influences. He cites Greta Thunberg, yet does not mention the assistance his company provided Thunberg (current We Don't Have Time special youth advisor and trustee) that would result in her campaign going international. Nor does he identify his relationship with Thunberg's mother, Marlena Ernman, who is briefly cited in the same article.

104 https://www.dn.se/debatt/den-akuta-klimatkrisen-kraver-bred-politisk-samling/
105 [Full letter in English]: https://medium.com/wedonthavetime/a-broad-political-consensus-is-needed-to-achieve-a-sustainable-future-ffecad1e58f7
106 https://www.globalutmaning.se/styrelse/anders-wijkman/
107 https://miljo-utveckling.se/ingmar-rentzhog-ar-arets-miljoinfluencer-2018/

> **Can you mention three influences that you follow daily?**
>
> - Eric Holthaus, Pär Holmgren and Greta Thunberg.
>
> Funny that you mention Greta Thunberg, because she came second in the price.
>
> - Then I am even happier for the price. What she does is amazing. And this is a brilliant example of how it is about helping each other. I helped her when she was not so big on social media and now she can help me as she is more famous than me globally, concludes Ingmar Rentzhog.

Earlier in the year, on May 4, 2018,[108] Rentzhog and Ernman were both featured guests at the Friday opening gala of the climate conference[109] ("climate change day") held on May 4-6 in Stockholm, Sweden. Greta Thunberg's sister, Beata Ernman-Thunberg, was also featured in the program. This was a low-key, modest event.[110]

108 https://klimataktion.se/2018/05/06/klimatriksdagen-selyssna-pa-foredragen/
109 https://www.youtube.com/watch?v=ivrMBLPKBwM
110 https://www.facebook.com/klimatriksdagen/photos/a.522165474544682/1817832918311258/?type=3&theater

**17.20 Samtal om kapitalets makt och påverkan på klimatet.**
**Konferencier Pia Björnstrand, talesperson Klimataktion och advokat**
På scen möter vi också:

***Aaron Maltaise,*** statsvetare och forskare inom hållbar finans vid Stockholm Environment Institute samt ansvarig för forskningen i det nystartade Stockholm Sustainable Finance Centre.

***Ingmar Rentzhog,*** initiativtagare till We Don't Have Time, ett socialt nätverk som verkar för att sätta press på politiker och företagsledare att skynda på klimatomställningen.

***Frida Arevik,*** rådgivare på Fossil Free Sweden där hon verkar för att Sveriges AP-fonder ska få en mer hållbar profil.

***Karl-Henrik Robért,*** professor och grundare av Naturliga Steget som verkat för att främja forskning inom hållbarhet i över 25 år.

***Åsa Wallenberg,*** vd SPP Fonder.

**17.50 Mingel, fortsatta samtal och lättare förtäring**

**19.00 Klimatriksdagens invigningsgala börjar**
Bland gästerna finner vi ***Malena Ernman*** (2018 års Grammisvinnare som årets hållbara artist), ***Marit Bergman*** (Grammis- och P3-guld-vinnare),

Thunberg was born into privilege and wealth.

Her mother is Swedish opera singer and celebrity Malena Ernman. Her father is actor Svante Thunberg, while her grandfather is actor and director Olof Thunberg. "Her ancestor on her father's side is the Nobel Prize winner, Svante Arrhenius. Arrhenius was a Swedish physicist and chemist who received the Nobel Prize for Chemistry in 1903. He is known for myriad scientific contributions but it was his discovery that an increase in atmospheric carbon dioxide increase the Earth's surface temperature. That finding led to the conclusion that human-made carbon dioxide emissions cause global warming."[111] [On the Influence of Carbonic Acid in the Air upon the Temperature of the Ground, Svante Arrhenius, 1896][112]

111 https://heavy.com/news/2018/12/greta-thunberg/
112 http://www.rsc.org/images/Arrhenius1896_tcm18-173546.pdf

The Svenska Dagbladet (SvD) is the third largest newspaper in circulation in Sweden. It has been generous in its coverage of both Thunberg and her mother, Ernman.

On May 30, 2018,[113] SvD selected Thunberg as one of its winning laureates in the SvD youth writing competition for the climate.

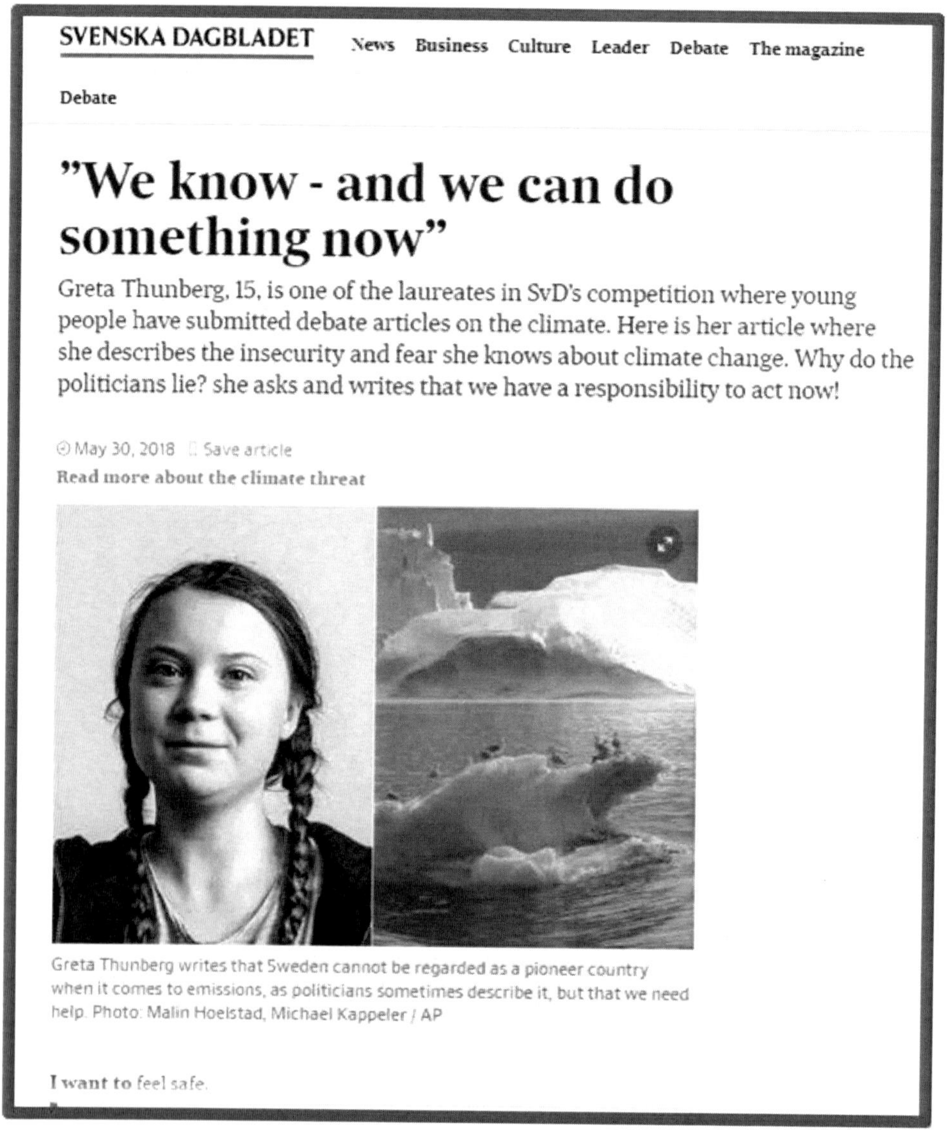

SVENSKA DAGBLADET  News  Business  Culture  Leader  Debate  The magazine

Debate

# "We know - and we can do something now"

Greta Thunberg, 15, is one of the laureates in SvD's competition where young people have submitted debate articles on the climate. Here is her article where she describes the insecurity and fear she knows about climate change. Why do the politicians lie? she asks and writes that we have a responsibility to act now!

May 30, 2018  Save article

**Read more about the climate threat**

Greta Thunberg writes that Sweden cannot be regarded as a pioneer country when it comes to emissions, as politicians sometimes describe it, but that we need help. Photo: Malin Hoelstad, Michael Kappeler / AP

**I want to** feel safe.

113 https://www.svd.se/vi-vet--och-vi-kan-gora-nagot-nu

Prior to this, on April 21, 2018,[114] SvD gave coverage of the family's book that was underway. The book "Scener ur Hjärtat"[115] (which translates into English as "Scenes of the Heart"), about the mental health challenges within her family coupled with anxieties facing climate change, would be launched on August 24, 2018, four days following the first day of Thunberg's school strike (August 20, 2018).

SVENSKA DAGBLADET News Business Culture Leader Debate The magazine

Sweden

# Greta's health was the start of Ernman's climate fight

When the family crashed, the Ernman / Thunberg family seriously got their eyes on the climate threat. Now they write a self-disclosing book about global warming, economic gaps and mental ill-health - all symptoms of the acute sustainability crisis we humans are in.

By Jenny Stiernstedt 21 apr, 2018 Save article

**Read more about the Climate competition**

Greta Thunberg 15 years old is the daughter of Malena Ernman and runs her parents in the struggle for the climate. Photo: Malin Hoelstad

**Young people are the group** in society that is most concerned about climate change, according to survey after examination. A fact that has been especially

**Top News**

**Löfven: The agreem - it does not move**
SWEDEN 3 tim

**M: "C and L support go in opposition"**
SWEDEN Today 04.

**19th century house "Have always wonde**
SWEDEN Today 02.

**"You get happier wh train"**
SWEDEN 1 tim

**Important laws aga terrorism in progre**
SWEDEN 3 tim

RELATED TOPICS

Mental illness

Burnout

Malena Ernman

The climate threat

114 https://www.svd.se/gretas-halsa-blev-starten-for-ernmans-klimatkamp
115 https://www.dn.se/kultur-noje/malena-ernman-vi-branner-ut-oss-pa-en-utbrand-planet/

World Wildlife Fund (WWF), perhaps the most corporate and egregious NGO[116] in the world, and a fully corporatized Greenpeace, have both been instrumental in the propping up of Thunberg with the support of other international NGOs such as 350.org. On October 11, 2017, WWF Sweden awarded Ernman[117] with the Environmental Hero award.

On September 17, 2018,[118] WWF Sweden named Thunberg as one of its three nominees for the Young Environmental Hero of the year 2018.

Greenpeace Sweden: "Malena Ernman is an incredible activist in the fight to preserve our forest for future generations. Thanks to the support of her, and all of you other amazing people who support us, we can continue to protect our outstanding planet. Do you also want to give away a Christmas present that makes a real difference?"

[119] Greenpeace also utilizes Ernman, and Thunberg,[120] to promote their powerful brand. Few are aware that in 1997, Greenpeace believed that climate policy must reflect the understanding that the world must not exceed a 1ºC temperature rise.[121] Yet not long after, in 2009, with a full ecological crisis now engulfing the planet, Greenpeace led the demand (at the United Nations Conference of the Parties in Copenhagen), for a binding agreement that would allow the Earth to further warm to a full 2ºC. The 2ºC demand, under the umbrella group TckTckTck, co-founded by Greenpeace, would undermine[122] Bolivia, the G77 and other small island states that had fought for a binding agreement to keep global temperatures from exceeding 1ºC. The following year, 350.org – another co-founder of TckTckTck – would undermine the Indigenous peoples of Bolivia yet again[123] at the World People's Conference on Climate Change and the Rights of Mother Earth, held in Cochabamba, Bolivia.

116 https://www.dailymotion.com/video/x105tsl
117 https://www.wwf.se/press/aktuellt/1717443-arets-miljohjaltar-utsedda-av-wwf
118 https://www.wwf.se/press/pressrum/pressmeddelanden/1748099-nio-nominerade-till-arets-miljohjalte-2018
119 https://www.facebook.com/greenpeace.sverige/photos/a.142619071890/10154962379996891/?type=1&theater
120 https://www.greenpeace.org/international/story/20165/5-young-activists-who-inspired-us-this-year/
121 http://academia.edu/3880272/Greenpeace_International_Cites_Maximum_1C_UNAGGG_October_1_1997
122 http://www.theartofannihilation.com/the-most-important-cop-briefings-that-no-one-ever-heard-truth-lies-racism-omnicide/
123 http://www.theartofannihilation.com/category/articles-2014/350-agent-saboteur/

## "CAPITALISM IS IN DANGER OF FALLING APART"

> *"But the more important fact remains: the mainstream debate is about how to practise capitalism, not whether we should choose between capitalism and some other system." — Generation Investment*

"We are making the case for long-term greed." Al Gore and David Blood, in Generation's New York City Office. August 25, 2015. (Christopher Griffith)
124

Utilizing the power of celebrity (an unprecedented phenomenon for the expansion of capital in the West), today's global influencers such as Thunberg are fully utilized to create a sense of urgency in regard to the climate crisis. The unspoken reality is, they are the very marketing strategy to save capitalism. This is a very "inconvenient truth".

124 https://www.theatlantic.com/magazine/archive/2015/11/the-planet-saving-capitalism-subverting-surprisingly-lucrative-investment-secrets-of-al-gore/407857/

The Financial Times, July 27, 2014:

> *"Now is a crucial moment for investors, he continues. "The next five to 10 years is the most critical time to accelerate the transition to a low-carbon economy.* ***We think capitalism is in danger of falling apart.*** *As a result, the business, which has been fairly reticent in the past about the mechanics of investing sustainably, is planning to increase its visibility.* ***'We need to go all in. We are going to be more aggressive because we have to.'"***
> *— Blood and Gore: "Capitalism is in Danger of Falling Apart", Financial Times, July 27, 2014*[125]

The September 8, 2015[126] article "David Blood and Al Gore Want to Reach the Next Generation", published by Institutional Investor, disclosed that "the California State Teachers' Retirement System [CalSTRS], the second-largest public pension fund in the U.S., with $191 billion in assets, was the first American institutional investor to invest in Generation." This was part and parcel of the divestment campaign led by Ceres partner 350.org on behalf of Wall Street and finance. Jack Ehnes, CEO of CalSTRS,[127] also serves on the board of Ceres.

The same article sheds light on the driving force behind the environmental NGOs that comprise the non-profit industrial complex and interlocking directorate highway that merges the non-profit industrial complex (NPIC) with the corporate world of finance:

> *"I would highly recommend people who are looking to divest from carbon take a look at Generation,' says* ***Larry Schweiger, a longtime conservationist and a board member of the Climate Reality Project****, a nonprofit founded by Gore to promote education and initiatives about climate change.* ***Schweiger was president and CEO of the National Wildlife Federation from 2004 to 2014; under his watch the NWF became a Generation investor. 'It was one of the best-performing investments in our portfolio****.' he says." — September 8, 2015,*[128] *"David Blood and Al Gore Want to Reach the Next Generation, Institutional Investor"*

125 https://www.ft.com/content/9fe06a2a-11b7-11e4-8279-00144feabdc0
126 https://www.institutionalinvestor.com/article/b14z9wt9vk3ycy/david-blood-and-al-gore-want-to-reach-the-next-generation
127 https://www.calstrs.com/profile/jack-ehnes
128 https://www.institutionalinvestor.com/article/b14z9wt9vk3ycy/david-blood-and-al-gore-want-to-reach-the-next-generation

Jumping forward to April 29, 2018, the article *Al Gore: Sustainability is History's Biggest Investment Opportunity,* published by the Financial Times, discloses "climate wealth" is not for the many, but rather for the few:

> *"Generation lists large public sector investors among its clients, such as Calstrs, the $223bn Californian teachers' pension plan, the $192bn New York State pension plan and the UK's Environment Agency retirement fund.* ***It also manages money for wealthy individuals but has stopped short of opening to retail investors. Almost all its assets are run in equity mandates, yet $1bn is invested in private equity."***[129]

> *"I called Generation Income and found that their investment opportunities are limited. They have two investment funds – Global Equity and Asia Equity.* ***The Global Equity fund is currently closed – there is a multi-year waiting list that is also currently closed. The minimum investment is $1 million and you need to be super-accredited.*** *The fund seems to be targeted at institutional investors – not individuals. The Asia Equity fund is open but* ***the same minimum requirements apply ($1M minimum)****."* [130]

Generation Investment board members include eco-luminaries such as Mary Robinson, a former president of Ireland and the founder of the non-profit Mary Robinson Foundation. Robinson serves as president to Richard Branson's B Team, which is managed by Purpose – the public relations arm of Avaaz. At this juncture, seeing as we are being led to believe that "sustainable investments" are the pathway to solving our planetary crisis, it might be wise to ask in what sustainable corporations Generation Investment is investing. Generation Investment has created a focus list of some 125

February 9, 2007: Sir Richard Branson (L) and former vice-president of the United States of America, Al Gore pose at the launch of The Virgin Earth Challenge in London. The challenge is for a USD 25M science and technology prize fund for viable products to remove at least 1 billion tons of atmospheric carbon dioxide per year. (Photo by Bruno Vincent/Getty Images)

129 https://www.ft.com/content/1757dc40-486f-11e8-8ee8-cae73aab7ccb
130 https://aiofinancial.com/generation-investment-management/

companies around the world in which it invests not based on how sustainable the business is, but rather, "on the quality of their business and management."[131]

Generation Investment's portfolio and investments include multinational corporations with horrendous records of malfeasance, such as Amazon, Nike, Colgate, MasterCard, and the Chipotle restaurant chain,[132] with heavy investments in health and technology.[133] And as all of these corporations are heavily invested and/or dependent on fossil fuels, how Generation Investment can justify investing in these companies is anyone's guess.

> *"[Gore] and his colleagues are aiming at a small audience within the financial world that steers the flow of capital, and at the political authorities that set the rules for the financial system.* ***'It turns out that in capitalism, the people with the real influence are the ones with capital!'*** *Gore told me during one of our talks this year. The message he hopes Generation's record will call attention to is one the world's investors can't ignore: They can make more money if they change their practices in a way that will, at the same time, also reduce the environmental and social damage* ***modern capitalism*** *can do."* [134]

> *"It's about an industrial transformation on a scale that we've never seen before." — Sharan Burrow, general secretary, International Trade Union Confederation, B Team leader*[135]

> *"This is the biggest economic opportunity of our lifetime. This movement has left the station and is never going to stop." — Jean Oelwang, President, Virgin Unite, Senior Partner, The B Team*

131 https://www.institutionalinvestor.com/article/b14z9wt9vk3ycy/david-blood-and-al-gore-want-to-reach-the-next-generation
132 https://finance.yahoo.com/news/already-48-2018-bill-ackman-040808960.html
133 https://www.bloomberg.com/news/articles/2019-01-04/genetic-analysis-firm-gets-77-million-to-fund-growth-eyes-ipo
134 http://www.resilientinvestor.com/al-gore-sri/
[Tracking Al Gore's Generation Investment Management Portfolio: https://www.nasdaq.com/quotes/institutional-portfolio/generation-investment-management-llp-733957]
135 https://vimeo.com/219534514

Above: The Washington D.C, 2017 People's Climate March: "The B Team, led by Sir Richard Branson, Sharan Burrow and former Vice President Al Gore, joined hundreds of thousands of workers, scientists, business leaders, students, parents, grandparents, children and indigenous groups demanding action on climate change by the U.S. administration." [136]

136 http://www.bteam.org/plan-b/restore-nature/b-team-joins-peoples-climate-march-for-jobs-and-justice/

## AN INCONVENIENT CASE STUDY: M-KOPA SOLAR, AFRICA

Source: M-Kopa website

> *"We think it's possible to build a business with no trade-offs. We can benefit the environment. Our customers will be better off. And we'll get richer. We all can win." — M-Kopa Canadian co-founder, Jesse Moore*

Gore, with a net worth of approx. 350 million US dollars,[137] pays much lip service to subjects of inequality, wealth disparity and poverty. Thus, it is useful to actually take a look at what the much-hyped green energy revolution actually looks like, when played out in real life and exactly who is being served by the so-called "green revolution".

137 https://www.thewealthrecord.com/celebs-bio-wiki-salary-earnings-2019-2020-2021-2022-2023-2024-2025/politician/al-gore-net-worth/

M-Kopa Solar – "Power for Everyone" is a pay-per-use solar power provider (in the form of solar kits) created for impoverished African countries by white uber-rich capitalists. The countries targeted thus far include rural Kenya, Tanzania and Uganda.

M-Kopa is the brainchild of Jesse Moore (CEO), Chad Larson and Nick Hughes — who helped develop M-Pesa, which has more than 19 million users in Kenya.[138]

From its inception, Gore's firm has been a lead equity investor[139] of M-Kopa. Incubated by Signal Point Partners in 2011, M-Kopa Solar raised money from investors including Richard Branson and Generation Investment Management.

138 M-Pesa is a mobile phone-based money transfer, financing and microfinancing service. It was launched in 2007 by Vodafone for Safaricom and Vodacom (the largest mobile network operators in Kenya and Tanzania). It has expanded to Afghanistan, South Africa, India, Romania, and Albania.) In Kenya, M-Pesa is being utilized to impose a debt ideology/familiarity that reflects western debt ideology. https://www.cio.co.ke/m-pesa-fuliza-lends-upto-ksh-1bn-in-8-days-after-launch/

139 http://solar.m-kopa.com/about/investors/

Launching in late 2012, the company's initial goal of selling 1,000 solar packages a week within three years was reached within 12 months. On December 2, 2015, M-Kopa, now the world's leading "pay-as-you-go energy provider to off-grid homes", announced the closing of a 19 million USD financing round led by Generation Investment Management LLP.[140]

Included on the M-Kopa board of advisors[141] is Colin Le Duc, a founding partner of Generation Investment Management and the Co-CIO of Generation's growth equity Climate Solutions Funds.

Other investors/lenders/partners[142] include Shell Foundation and the Bill and Melinda Gates Foundation.

At this juncture, before we continue, it is vital to note that, in 2015, M-Kopa estimated that eighty percent of its customers lived on less than 2 USD per day.

By 2015, M-Kopa had reached over USD 40 million in revenue.

The December 2, 2015 Bloomberg article[143] "The Solar Company Making a Profit on Poor Africans – M-Kopa Plans to be a $1 Billion Company by Selling Solar Panels to Rural Residents—and Providing Them With Credit" discloses the reality behind corporate vulturism hidden beneath a vellum of white saviour greenwash. Following the "success"[144] of prepaid water meters[145] for many African countries, M-Kopa charges high interest rates to the poor, with astronomically higher dividends/returns going back to the rich:

> *"**The interest M-Kopa charges is high by U.S. or European standards. The cash price of one of its products is about 20 percent less than the installment price**. But in the markets where the company's working—so far, Kenya, Tanzania, and Uganda—the rates are competitive. **Traditional microfinance companies typically charge about 20 percent interest on their loans, and in October the Kenyan government issued treasury bills that offered investors a 23 percent annual return.**"*

Upon first glance, a person would assume this business is the selling of solar. Yet this assumption would be a mistake. The product is finance: "About a quarter of those who pay off their first purchase move on to others, the company

140 http://www.m-kopa.com/generation-investment-management-leads-19m-equity-round-in-m-kopa-solar/
141 http://solar.m-kopa.com/our-board/
142 http://solar.m-kopa.com/about/investors/
143 https://www.bloomberg.com/features/2015-mkopa-solar-in-africa/
144 https://www.afrik21.africa/en/niger-citytaps-raises-e-1-million-and-signs-with-veolia-africa-for-prepaid-water/
145 https://www.namibian.com.na/176678/archive-read/Residents-reject-prepaid-water-meters

says." This is colonization in a 21st century new form. Colonization via debt made possible by the selling of Western values.

Other vultures exploiting the impoverished and vulnerable under the guise of green and "clean energy for all" include stalwart organizations, such as the Gates Foundation and Mastercard.

Unlike Western finance, where loans are usually paid in monthly installments, Africans are not given this same measure of trust. Rather, on top of a deposit, they must pay for their new loan (debt) on a daily basis. Perhaps this can be filed under "green energy racism". Those that do not make their payments, will be punished accordingly: "Our loan officer is that SIM card in the device that can shut it off remotely," says Chad Larson, M-Kopa's finance director and its third co-founder. "We know that it's important for them to keep their lights on at night, so they can be counted on to keep paying."[146] ["The pay-as-you-go feature is enabled by embedded machine-to-machine technology that allows M-KOPA to receive payments through the M-Pesa mobile money platform. M-KOPA can turn off the device remotely if the customer falls behind on payments. Repayments create a credit history for poor consumers that may give them access to other financial services."][147]

> *"The solar lamps are programmed in such a way that they automatically switch off whenever customers default on the daily payments. The start-up provides a solar power system that consists of a panel, three lamps, radio and mobile phone charging kit." — M-Pesa solar dealer to blacklist defaulters with credit bureaus, February 18, 2015*[148]

Daily payments for M-Kopa are topped up through the M-Pesa service whereby Safaricom, the largest telecommunications company in Kenya (and the most profitable company in the East and Central African region), earns an undisclosed fee for every transaction. M-Kopa and Kenya Power are Safaricom's biggest pay-billing clients. [In 2015, Kenya's Safaricom CEO Bob Collymore[149] was the fourth African to join Richard Branson's B Team – Ventures Africa].

> *"We don't invest in solar at all," says David Rossow, who helps manage the Gates Foundation's $1.5 billion portfolio of program-related investments (PRIs). The foundation doesn't even have a clean energy program. But it does have a program called Finan-*

146 https://www.bloomberg.com/features/2015-mkopa-solar-in-africa/
147 https://ssir.org/articles/entry/banking_on_the_poor
148 https://www.businessdailyafrica.com/Corporate-News/M-Pesa-solar-dealer-to-blacklist-defaulters-with-credit-bureaus/539550-2628252-p0gnpfz/index.html
149 http://venturesafrica.com/kenyas-safaricom-ceo-becomes-the-fourth-african-to-join-the-b-team/

*cial Services for the Poor. "We care about asset-backed lending for the last mile."* [150]

Of further value for our white saviour entrepreneurs is the valuable metadata: "M-Kopa's current customer contract stipulates that the data the company amasses can be used only to improve customer experience, but the company has plans to collect listener and viewership data from its radios and televisions. 'There's data we can gather that practically no one else can', [Chad] Larson says."

And what does the green energy revolution, wholly dependent on the further plundering of the Earth, actually bring to Africa, where more than 600 million people have zero access to electricity and more than 300 million have no clean sanitation? A solar oven? A toilet? Water filtration? Plumbing? Schools? Health clinics? Hospitals? Answer: the television.

*"Make your payments in full and on time, so you can qualify for system upgrades and much more!" — M-Kopa website*

And just because the business is actually finance, more than it is providing solar products,[151] [2] that doesn't mean there isn't ample opportunity to rob African people blind.[152] The price of the basic 24-inch television solar kit [2-1] [2-2] when financed is an outrageous 644.88 USD. The cash price is still a whopping 546.61 USD, which is an exorbitant sum for people who exist on $2 (USD) per day. Of course, this price only remains so if the daily payments are made each and every day, ensuring no additional interest or penalties accumulate on top of the original loan amount.

The gross exploitation here is beyond the pale. Consider a 30W solar package comparable to the M-Kopa package above can be purchased retail for 157.99 USD on Amazon.[153] Likewise, the price of a basic 24-inch LED television is of-

150 https://ssir.org/articles/entry/banking_on_the_poor
151 http://www.m-kopa.com/products/
152 The company M-KOPA offers the following three(3) product packages:
[2-1] The M-KOPA 5 Solar Home System can be purchased with a deposit of $2,999.00 Ksh. ($29.75 USD), plus 420 daily payments of $50.00 Ksh($0.50 USD). This total payment, including the deposit, is $23,999.00 Ksh. ($238.03 USD). The cash purchase price with no financing is $18,999.00 Ksh. ($188.44 USD). [Accessed January 27, 2019]
The "M-KOPA 5 Solar Home System" includes one 8W solar panel, one rechargeable radio, one M-KOPA 5 control unit with a lithium battery, four 1.2W LED bulbs, one 5-in-1 phone charge cable, one custom charge cable, and one rechargeable LED torch.
[2-2] The M-KOPA 600 requires a deposit of $5,999.00 UGX. ($59.50 USD), plus 590 daily payments of $100.00 Ksh($0.99 USD). The total payment, including the deposit, is $64,999.00 Ksh. ($644.68 USD). The cash purchase price with no financing is $ 1,999,000.00 Ksh. ($546.61 USD)." [Accessed January 27, 2019]
The "M-KOPA 600 (24 TV)" package includes one M-KOPA 600 control unit, one 24-inch flat screen digital TV, one 30W solar panel, one TV remote control, one TV aerial, two solar lights, one solar rechargeable LED torch, one solar rechargeable radio, and two phone charging cables. "Satellite Dish & CAM Card provided separately."
[2-3] The M-KOPA 600 w/ Zuku CAM requires a deposit of $6,999.00 UGX. ($69.42 USD), plus 590 daily payments of $135.00 Ksh. ($1.34 USD). The total payment, including the deposit, is $86,649.00 Ksh. ($859.42 USD). The cash purchase price with no financing is $ 69,999.00 Ksh. ($694.27 USD)." [Accessed January 27, 2019]
153 https://www.amazon.com/Foldable-HKYH-Lighting-Charger-Emergency/dp/B013BBD70O

ten advertised in the United States and Canada for under 100.00 USD/CND. Many of the items sold in the packages [2-3] can be found in the proliferating Western "dollar" stores for $1.00 USD each.

Photo: M-Kopa

One might wonder what happens when the loans outlive the outsourced products with short-lived warranties – a two-year warranty on the 24-inch television and a one-year warranty on accessories.

Between bombing campaigns on African countries, former US president Barack Obama found time to visit the M-Kopa solar corporation. "US President Barack Obama talks to June Muli, M-Kopa's head of customer care, during the Global Entrepreneurship Summit in Nairobi in July 2015. Photo: M-Kopa." [154]

154 https://www.forbes.com/sites/tobyshapshak/2016/01/28/how-kenyas-m-kopa-brings-prepaid-solar-power-to-rural-africa/#3cd441a52dbf

In February 2015, M-Kopa announced its plan to have their customers, who defaulted on their loans, blacklisted with credit bureaus:

> *"M-Pesa-linked solar dealer, M-Kopa, will from April begin sharing information on loan defaulters with credit reference bureaus to arrest the rising number of non-payers. The firm has issued a notice saying it plans to share information on how customers pay for their M-Kopa solar kits, in a move that will see defaulters blacklisted by lenders. M-Kopa now joins other utility providers such as Kenya Power and water service boards which have taken to credit reference bureaus to list those who default on paying their bills."*[155]

Credit and the perpetual debt that ensues is not the only aspect of the American dream that multinational corporations are bringing to the Global South.

To be clear, it's not "sustainable economies" that our corporate overlords pursue. A capitalism that is in trouble, must seek out – in order to save itself, new markets:[156]

> *"The Gates Foundation's team saw in M-KOPA an opportunity to demonstrate that mobile financial services could help businesses get more such valuable products into the hands of a new market of eager consumers: poor people."* [157]

> *"The key was helping M-KOPA turn its customer accounts into bankable collateral. Other investors were taking equity positions in the startup. The Gates Foundation instead made a $5 million loan, alongside the Commercial Bank of Africa.*[158] *The thesis:* ***if M-KOPA could successfully pay back the loan, local commercial banks would see the payments from pay-as-you-go financing schemes as a reliable revenue stream. That would create a new lendable asset class." — Banking on the Poor****, summer, 2016, Stanford Social Innovation Review*[159]

Here, we must look at the reality behind the "green jobs" – that M-Kopa created – a pivotal selling feature of the so-called "green economy", Green New

155 https://www.businessdailyafrica.com/Corporate-News/M-Pesa-solar-dealer-to-blacklist-defaulters-with-credit-bureaus/539550-2628252-p0gnpfz/index.html
156 https://www.azuri-technologies.com/news/azuri-partners-with-zuku-launches-solar-powered-paygo-tv-and-satellite-service
157 https://ssir.org/articles/entry/banking_on_the_poor
158 http://cbagroup.com/
159 https://ssir.org/articles/entry/banking_on_the_poor

Deal, sustainable development / global goals, and a myriad of other holistic sounding language that mask reality.

What is rarely mentioned, if ever, is the fact that the M-Kopa solar panels, televisions, etc. are not made locally. Rather, they are "sourced from overseas markets" (China). Although the company has suggested that solar panels may be made locally over the next few years (likely due to the growing animosity from Kenyans) the following information will demonstrate that this will only be the case if Kenyans can be exploited more so than Chinese.

Chad Larson, co-founder and finance director of M-Kopa Solar, poses for a photograph at the headquarters of M-Kopa Solar in Nairobi, Kenya, on Wednesday, July 22, 2015. Customers agree to pay for the solar panel with regular instalments which M-Kopa, a Nairobi-based provider of solar-lighting systems, then monitors for payments that are made using a mobile-phone money-transfer service. Photographer: Waldo Swiegers/Bloomberg via Getty Images

In the March 19, 2018[160] article, "Solar Firm M-Kopa Lays off 450 Staff to Cut Costs", published by Business Daily Africa, the reason for doing so was disclosed in no uncertain terms:

> *"Kenya's mobile phone-based solar kit reseller* ***M-Kopa Solar fired 450 workers in its subsidiaries in four countries to ease operational costs and boost profitability.***

160 https://www.businessdailyafrica.com/markets/marketnews/Solar-firm-M-Kopa-lays-off-450-staff-to-cut-costs/3815534-4348416-561ghj/index.html

*M-Kopa co-founder and CEO Jesse Moore said the firm was in a better position to meet its targets and expand solar connections to the next one million customers in Kenya, Uganda and Tanzania offices.*
*'This was done to reduce fixed costs and keep us on the path to profitability which resulted in job reductions across offices in Kenya, Uganda, Tanzania and UK, reducing our global headcount by 18 per cent,' he said."*

An article published by Quartz Africa four days prior, on March 15, 2018,[161] was even more to the point:

> *"M-Kopa, the Kenyan pay-per-use solar power provider, is downsizing in a bid to improve its competitiveness, ensure long-term sustainability,* ***and increase return for investors****."*

This is worth emphasizing. To be clear – this is a profitable increase for investors, with net-worths of millions of dollars – made at the expense of firing workers making approx. $2.00 USD per day.

March 15, 2018: M-KOPA secures 100 Ksh million from CDC, FinDev Canada: CIO East Africa (L-R) Jesse Moore, co-Founder and CEO, M-KOPA and Paul Lamontagne, managing director of FinDev Canada during a customer site visit in Ngong. [162]

161 https://qz.com/africa/1229170/m-kopa-solar-lays-off-kenya-uganda-staff-as-it-restructures/
162 https://www.cio.co.ke/m-kopa-secures-ksh100million-from-cdc-findev-canada/

Immediately following the sacking of African M-Kopa employees – along with outsourcing – Generation Investment put up more funding. The March 21, 2018[163] article "M-Kopa Solar Receives $10 Million Investment After Sacking 150 Employees" published by the Kenyan Wall Street, disclosed the following:

> *"The investment comes after the company completed* ***a restructuring exercise that saw staff count reduce by 18% from 1000 to 850 across East Africa****. As we reported last week,[164] about* ***78 developers were fired and their work has now been outsourced to a foreign company called Applicita[165] that is owned by the company's new CTO.***
>
> *According to the CEO Jesse Moore, the restructuring process has been driven by the need to increase its competitiveness, enhance long-term sustainability, and* ***boost investors' returns.***
>
> *The FinDev investment was led by CDC Group, an investor that had formerly pumped $7 million into the company, and includes follow-on investments by Generation Investment Management and LGT Venture Philanthropy. The two firms are current M-Kopa shareholders."*

The white colonization that continues to proliferate was not lost on Kenyan Wall Street, which noted:

> *"...****the company continues to raise eyebrows over its status as a Kenyan startup since its senior management is mostly composed of foreigners. What's more, the matter of sacking local employees to outsource its operations to a foreign company will not go forgotten.****"*

163 https://kenyanwallstreet.com/m-kopa-solar-receives-10-million-investment-after-sacking-150-employees/
164 http://kenyanwallstreet.com/m-kopa-solar-fires-18-of-its-staff-including-all-developers-outsources-work-to-a-foreign-company-linked-to-new-cto
165 https://www.applicita.com/

## "THE GATHERING" & NURTURING OF FOUNDATION-FUNDED PRAGMATISM

As disclosed in ACT I of this series, the very first people tagged in the initial Thunberg school strike tweet by We Don't Have Time founder, Ingmar Rentzhog, were the following five Twitter users: Greta Thunberg, This Is Zero Hour, Jamie Margolin,[166] the teenage founder of This Is Zero Hour, Al Gore's Climate Reality Project and the People's Climate Strike[167] Twitter account (in the identical font and aesthetics as 350.org).

The first tweets from any given NGO Twitter accounts are important, as they often reveal exactly for what purpose or action the account was created. In this particular instance, the very first tweet from the People's Climate Strike account contained the hashtag #floodthesystem (July 24, 2015). This hashtag was devised to promote the action named Flood Wall Street, which took place on September 28, 2015, leading up to the second People's Climate March on November 29, 2015. In 2015, the first started using the #floodthesystem hashtag were: This Changes Everything (NGO of Naomi Klein, 350.org board member), May 6, 2015;[168] OccuWorld, May 12, 2015[169] ("something big is coming this fall"), retweeted by Rising Tide North America, Sharon Vardatira, Meridian Consulting, May 13, 2015[170] and Occupy Wall Street, May 20, 2015.[171]

The strategy behind devising different social media accounts affiliated with hashtags, campaigns and NGO manufactured movements, is one that will catch fire. Such is the case with the Climate Strike[172] (#climatestrike) Twitter account (Climate Strike! – Global Climate Convergence[173] that was largely abandoned by 2017), and #EarthStrike, which largely failed to

166 https://www.teenvogue.com/story/jamie-margolin-21-under-21-2018
167 https://twitter.com/Climate_Strike
168 https://twitter.com/thischanges/status/596070470207733760
169 https://twitter.com/OccuWorld/status/598276065883099136
170 https://twitter.com/MeridianAmherst/status/598477680544190464
171 https://twitter.com/OccupyWallStNYC/status/601024965727657984
172 https://globalclimateconvergence.org/climate-strike/
173 https://globalclimateconvergence.org/about/whoweare/

catch fire (thus far), to this very recent climate strike – as a hashtag – that has struck gold with the public psyche.

The "one 15 year old girl" tweet was then retweeted by Paola Fiore, founder and CEO of ETICAMBIENTE®[174] Sustainability Management & Communications Consulting. Fiore is also the National Coordinator for Italy for The Climate Reality Project Europe. Affiliations, memberships and partnerships of Fiore's firm include but are not limited to, the Association for Coaching,[175] Eco Community,[176] United Planet Faith & Science Initiative[177] (Archbishop Desmond Tutu is a founding member, as is Dr. Rajendra Pachauri), 2degrees[178] (funded by the European Commission), and the International Coach Federation.[179] ETICAMBIENTE® holds membership[180] with both The Climate Reality Project, and its client, the International Society of Sustainability Professionals.[181]

The first "follows", selected from any given NGO Twitter account are also important, as they often reveal who created the account – or those closest affiliated with the project. In this instance, the first two follows for the People's Climate Strike Twitter account[182] (created in June 2015) are Cheri Honkala[183] and the Poor People's Economic Human Rights Campaign[184] founded by Honkala. Honkala was the "Our Revolution"[185] endorsed candidate for Pennsylvania state representative (#WeAreThe197th) in 2017.

With the formation of the board[186] announced on August 29, 2016, the 2018 Our Revolution winning cand-

174 http://www.eticambiente.com/
175 https://www.associationforcoaching.com/
176 https://profiles.eco/eticambiente.eco
177 http://www.upfsi.org/about/
178 https://2degreesmarketing.com/2degrees/clients
179 https://coachfederation.org/
180 https://profiles.eco/eticambiente.eco
181 https://www.sustainabilityprofessionals.org/
182 https://twitter.com/Climate_Strike/following
183 https://twitter.com/CheriHonkala
184 http://economichumanrights.org/
185 https://ourrevolution.com/

idates included Bernie Sanders[187] and Alexandria Ocasio-Cortez.[188] On September 18, 2018, Our Revolution (OR) and the Progressive Democrats of America (PDA) announced a formal partnership established by both of the organizations national boards. "PDA is a grassroots political action committee, founded in 2004 to transform the Democratic Party and U.S. politics by electing progressives to federal office." The PDA National Advisory Board includes members of US Congress, documentary film maker Michael Moore, commentator Thom Hartmann, Medea Benjamin of Code Pink, and others of high liberal status.[189]

186 https://ourrevolution.com/press/our-revolution-announces-formation-of-board/
187 https://ourrevolution.com/candidates/bernie-sanders/
188 https://ourrevolution.com/candidates/alexandria-ocasio-cortez/
189 "The PDA National Advisory Board includes members of US Congress: Representatives Barbara Lee, Keith Ellison, Raul Grijalva, and James McGovern; as well as documentarian Michael Moore, Actress / Activist Mimi Kennedy, Rev. Dr. Rodney Sadler, Author Jim Hightower, and Radio Hosts / Authors Lila Garrett and Thom Hartmann. Activists Michael Lighty, Medea Benjamin, Steve Cobble, Kristin Cabral, Dr. Paul Song, M.D., Belen Sisa, and Professor Marjorie Cohn also serve on the PDA Advisory Board, which is chaired by the exemplary activist Donna Smith."
https://ourrevolution.com/press/our-revolution-and-progressive-democrats-america-announce-strategic-partnership/ [Full Board: https://ourrevolution.com/about/#board Accessed January 10, 2019]

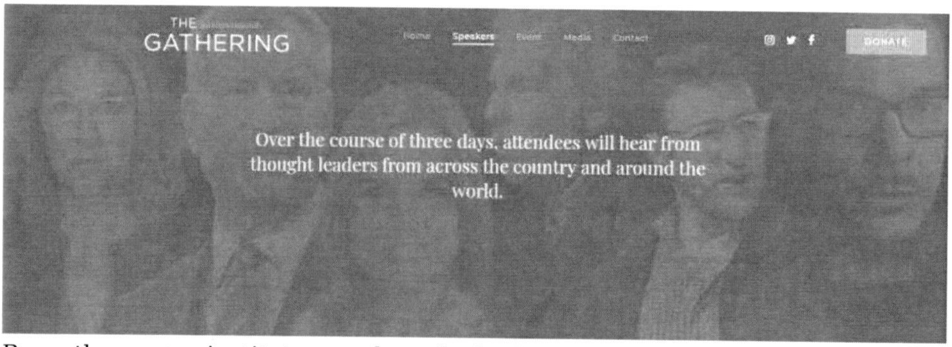


Recently, a new institute was launched which is partnered with Our Revolution:[190] The Sanders Institute[191] ("Our Mission: To Revitalize Democracy"). The inaugural conference (The Sanders Institute Gathering) took place in Burlington, Vermont (US) on November 29 – December 1, 2018. The invite-only event featured the crème de la crème of the liberal political establishment including: Bernie Sanders who delivered the keynote, 350.org board member Naomi Klein and 350.org founder Bill McKibben (Sanders Institute Fellow) who both spoke on the Green New Deal,[192] Jeffrey Sachs[193] (Sanders Institute Fellow), Cornel West (Sanders Institute Fellow) New York Mayor Bill de Blasio, Nina Turner (Ohio State Senator, president of Our Revolution), Ben Cohen (Ben & Jerry's), and U.S. representative Tulsi Gabbard[194] (Sanders Institute Fellow).[195]

The green bourgeoisie rubbed elbows with "celebrity activists" including Susan Sarandon, John Cusack, Danny Glover and Harry Belafonte (Glover and Belafonte are both Sanders Institute Fellows).[196] WCAX News reported[197] that the only debate that night was whether or not media would be allowed into the event. Ultimately, the media was given access to the event, but had to adhere to conditions of who they were, and who they were not allowed to record. (So much for freedom of the press.)

190 https://ourrevolution.com/
191 https://www.sandersinstitute.com/
192 http://www.wrongkindofgreen.org/2019/01/07/the-green-new-deal-has-an-afl-cio-problem/
193 http://deepdecarbonization.org/about/
194 https://www.congress.gov/bill/115th-congress/house-bill/3671/text
195 [Full list: https://sandersinstitutegathering.org/speakers/]
196 https://www.sandersinstitute.com/about/fellows
197 https://www.wcax.com/content/news/Progressive-thinkers-gather-for-Sanders-Institute-event-501587851.html

Participants spoke passionately about Indigenous rights, racism, etc. at the invite-only event of predominantly white rich saviours who are presented as the leaders of our only salvation. In reality, they are only trying to salvage a system (via reforms) in which they are flourishing. Another inconvenient truth at odds with the gathering are the promotional videos[198] produced for the institute, which deliberately strive to give the pretense of politically correct diversity and inclusion.[199] As previously highlighted, Zero Hour is one of the five Twitter accounts tagged in the first Thunberg school strike tweet. Partners of This Is Zero Hour[200] include: We Don't Have Time, 350.org, The Climate Reality Project, the Sierra Club, Power Shift, the Sunrise Movement and many other NGOs

July 20, 2018: Zero Hour's Jamie Margolin is to the left of Bernie Sanders (centre). Xiuhtezcatl Martinez is in the back row, far right. "Organizers with Zero Hour meet with Sen. Bernie Sanders during their lobbying day Thursday." Photo: Courtesy of Zero Hour

198 https://youtu.be/zbqmdWkK8ZI
199 Photo: https://earther.gizmodo.com/this-weekends-youth-climate-march-celebrates-diversity-1827729527
200 http://thisiszerohour.org/who-we-are/

that garner much power and influence within the non-profit industrial complex.

September 20, 2018, Twitter: "Thank you Vice President @algore for your support & endorsement of the #ThisIsZeroHour movement"

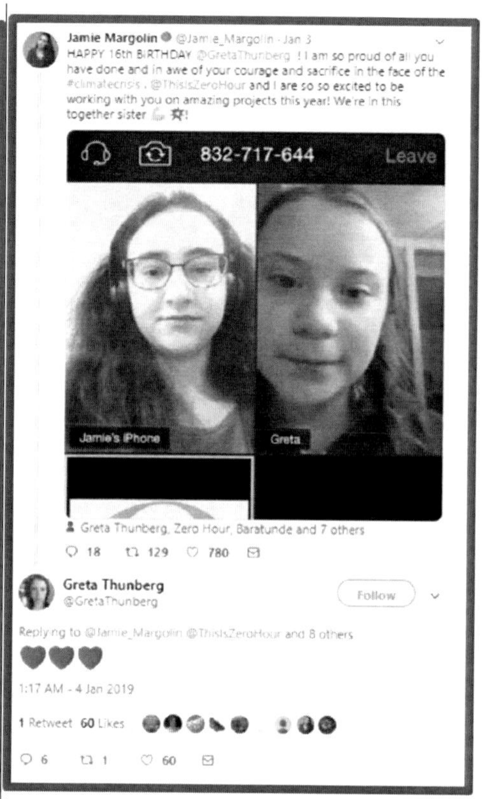

January 4, 2019, Twitter

In this December 10, 2018 tweet (9:35AM), ten Twitter accounts were tagged: 350.org, We Don't Have Time, the Sunrise Movement, Teen Vogue, Sierra Club, Greenpeace, Women's March, Our Children's Trust, Zero Hour, and March for Our Lives.
201

201 https://twitter.com/Jamie_Margolin/status/1072137242846486528

## ACTIVISM & CORPORATISM WORKING HAND-IN-HAND

The Climate Group is a co-founder of We Mean Business – a coalition of organizations working with thousands of the world's most powerful corporations and investors

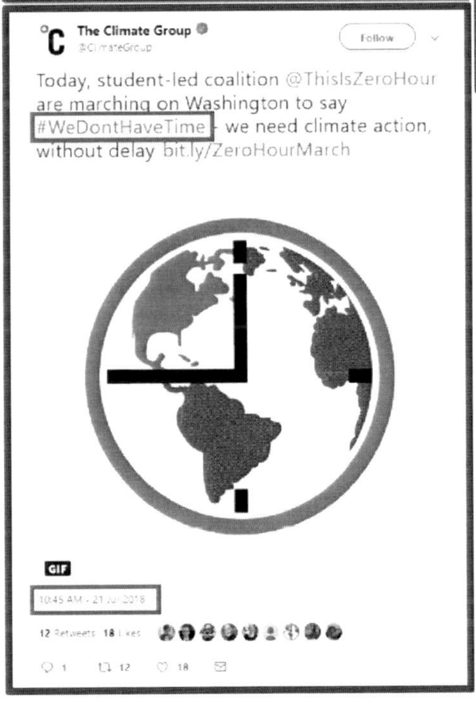


Perhaps the most noteworthy online exchange were the "words of encouragement" extended via Twitter by The Climate Group to Zero Hour for leading the Youth Climate March in July, 2018. Also of significance were the hashtags used in The Climate Group tweets: #WeDontHaveTime and #FrontlineYouth. This effectively illuminates the strategy and the key players behind the "climate movement" – where the NGOs, their funders, and the corporate entities are all on the same team.

This is not kindness. This is exquisite, albeit callous strategy.

Incubated by the Rockefeller Brothers Fund as an in-house project that later evolved into a free-standing institution, The Climate Group[202] is a co-founder of We Mean Business – "a coalition of organizations working with thousands of the world's most influential businesses and investors." The founding partners of We Mean Business[203] are: Business for Social Responsibility (BSR),[204] CDP[205] (formerly the Carbon Disclosure Project), Ceres,[206] The B Team,[207] The Climate Group,[208] The Prince of Wales's Corporate Leaders Group (CLG)[209] and World Business Council for Sustainable Development (WBCSD).[210] Together, these groups represent the most powerful – and ruthless – corporations on the planet, salivating to unleash 100 trillion US dollars for the fourth industrial revolution.

As I will demonstrate in the next segment of this series, the "frontline youth" energy is strategically being mobilized by a highly organized and sophisticated climate campaign. This same energy is being captured, then channeled back to save, strengthen and expand, the capitalist, hegemonic system that promises to destroy the future for these very same youth. One could call this a circular death economy. It takes much skill and co-ordination to "herd cats"[211] – to their own slaughter.

---

202 The Climate Group: The Rockefeller Brothers Fund also acts as an incubator for in-house projects that later evolve into free-standing institutions – a case in point being 'The Climate Group' (http://www.theclimate-group.org/), launched in London in 2004. The Climate Group coalition includes more than 50 of the world's largest corporations (http://www.theclimategroup.org/our-members/#undefined) and sub-national governments, including big polluters such as energy giants BP and Duke Energy, as well as several partner organizations, one being that of the big NGO Avaaz. The Climate Group are advocates of unproven carbon capture and storage technology (CCS), nuclear power and biomass as crucial technologies for a low-carbon economy. The Climate Group works closely with other business lobby groups, including the International Emissions Trading Association (IETA), which works consistently to sabotage climate action. The Climate Group also works on other initiatives, one being that of the 'Voluntary Carbon Standard' (http://www.v-c-s.org/), a new global standard for voluntary offset projects (http://www.redd-monitor.org/2010/03/25/richard-sandor-junk-bonds-to-carbon-cop-out/). One marketing strategist company labeled the Climate Group's campaign 'Together' as "the best inoculation against greenwash". The Climate Group has operations in Australia, China, Europe, India, and North America. It was a partner to the 'Copenhagen Climate Council'.

203 http://www.wemeanbusinesscoalition.org/

204 https://www.bsr.org/ [full membership and associate members list: https://www.bsr.org/en/membership/member-list]

205 https://www.cdp.net/en-US/Pages/HomePage.aspx

206 http://www.ceres.org/

207 http://bteam.org/

208 http://www.theclimategroup.org/

209 http://www.cisl.cam.ac.uk/business-action

210 http://www.wbcsd.org/home.aspx

211 Forbes, September 25, 2014: *Leadership Lessons from The People's Climate March*: "With that as her model of leadership it is perhaps no surprise that so many cats have been so successfully herded. But there is more. The other leadership lesson is putting project before person." [http://www.theartofannihilation.com/under-one-bad-sky-tcktcktcks-2014-peoples-climate-march-this-changed-nothing/]

# ACT IV

## THE HOUSE IS ON FIRE! & THE 100 TRILLION DOLLAR RESCUE

### SHAPING A GLOBAL ARCHITECTURE IN THE AGE OF THE FOURTH INDUSTRIAL REVOLUTION

*"15 minutes of fame is short-lived media publicity or celebrity of an individual or phenomenon. The expression was inspired by Andy Warhol's words "In the future, everyone will be world-famous for 15 minutes", which appeared in the program for a 1968 exhibition of his work at the Moderna Museet in Stockholm, Sweden."* [212]

January 25, 2019: "Finally, we have to applaud the lineup for Thursday's lunchtime panel. Marc Benioff was joined on the stage by Jane Goodall, Bono, teen climate activist Greta Thunberg, diplomat and environmentalist Christiana Figueres, president & CEO of Sompo Holdings Kengo Sakurada, and will.i.am. What a crew." Photo by Jeff Elder [213]

212 Photographer Nat Finkelstein claimed credit for the expression, stating that he was photographing Warhol in 1966 for a proposed book. A crowd gathered trying to get into the pictures and Warhol supposedly remarked that everyone wants to be famous, to which Finkelstein replied, "Yeah, for about fifteen minutes, Andy." The phenomenon is often used in reference to figures in the entertainment industry or other areas of popular culture." [Wikipedia]

213 [Source: "The 10 Best Moments From Davos With Salesforce" https://www.salesforce.com/content/blogs/us/en/2019/01/salesforce-at-davos-recap.html]

As Greta Thunberg is the founding block of this particular story, revisiting Sweden with the above observation feels like a good place to start part IV of this series where we deconstruct the ongoing marketing campaign with the most recent activity.

Let's begin.

On Thursday January 24, 2019, Greta Thunberg took part in a lunch panel presented by Marc Benioff at the World Economic Forum (WEF) in Davos, Switzerland. Benioff is the CEO and founder of Salesforce, as well as a co-founder of Breakthrough Energy (nuclear) with Bill Gates and other kindred billionaires. Also on the panel were Jane Goodall (United Nations Messenger of Peace)[214], Bono (U2 lead singer and "activist"), "will.i.am" (Black Eyed Peas founder and "philanthropist") and the young Greta Thunberg who made the following statement:

> *"Some people say that the climate crisis is something that we will have created, but that is not true, because if everyone is guilty then no one is to blame. And someone is to blame, some people, some companies, some decision-makers in particular, have known exactly what priceless values they have been sacrificing to continue making unimaginable amounts of money. And I think many of you here today belong to that group of people."*[215]

Thunberg's words were quickly launched into the international stratosphere of global media outlets and social media.

CNN, January 25, 2019:[216]

> *"On Thursday, **Thunberg gave an impromptu speech** at a lunch with a star-studded guest list that included music stars Bono and Will.i.am, Salesforce CEO Marc Benioff, former Goldman Sachs President Gary Cohn, and an array of bankers and investors. **She roasted them.**"*

Here, it is vital to note the usage of language: *impromptu* and *roasted.*

214 https://redd-monitor.org/2018/04/06/jane-goodall-institutes-redd-project-in-tanzania-a-totalitarian-approach-to-conservation-that-led-to-increased-inequity-undermining-of-democracy-and-violent-evictions/

215 [Greta Thunberg @ Davos – Inconvenient Truths: https://www.youtube.com/watch?time_continue=40&v=ScgUS-dZNKxg]

216 https://www.cnn.com/2019/01/25/europe/greta-thunberg-davos-world-economic-forum-intl/index.html

France 24, January 25, 2019:[217]

> *"Some people say that the climate crisis is something that we have all created, but that is not true. Because if everyone is guilty then no one is to blame, and someone is to blame. Some people, some companies, and some decision-makers in particular, have known exactly what priceless values they have been sacrificing to continue to make unimaginable amounts of money. And I think that many of you here today belong to that group of people,'* ***she said in her impromptu speech, delivered without a moment's hesitation****."*

EZ News, January 27, 2019:[218]

> *"On Thursday,* ***Thunberg gave an impromptu speech*** *at a lunch with a star-studded guest list that included Salesforce CEO Marc Benioff, former Goldman Sachs president and Trump administration official Gary Cohn, musicians Bono and Will.i.am, and an array of bankers and investors."*

Pluralist, January 28, 2019:[219]

> *"Greta Thunberg reportedly took a 32-hour train from her home in Sweden to the Swiss retreat and camped out in zero degrees-Fahrenheit temperatures to deliver* ***an impromptu roast of the celebrities and economic titans.*** *In a speech at lunch, she accused the high-profile guests of causing the warming of the planet that they had spent the prior several days grandstanding about fixing."*

As demonstrated in the above talking points, there is much emphasis from the international media to establish the idea that Thunberg's speech was spontaneous. As we will illustrate, it was not. This is merely an example of effective storytelling being put into practise, as orchestrated by the NGOs and corporate alliances that are handling Thunberg.

On January 22, 2019, three days prior to the "impromptu speech" at the WEF, a video was uploaded to YouTube by Uphill Media. ["Uphill Media, is the continuation of Bernie2016 TV and Political Revolution TV. We are 501(c)(3)3 non-

217 https://www.france24.com/en/20190125-swedish-teenager-greta-thunberg-hold-world-leaders-accountable-climate-change
218 https://eznws.com/2019/01/27/greta-thunberg-took-a-32-hour-train-to-the-world-economic-forum/
219 https://pluralist.com/celebs-left-in-stunned-silence-after-young-girl-calls-out-elite-hypocrites-to-their-faces/

profit independent media network focused on informing the electorate through engagement on the Internet."][220]

In this video of Thunberg speaking, filmed prior to her traveling from Stockholm to Davos, the key talking points within the message[221] are almost verbatim to the "impromptu" speech at WEF:

January 22, 2019 video:[222]

> *"Some people say that the climate crisis is something that we all have created. But that is just another convenient lie. Because if everyone is guilty then no one is to blame. And someone is to blame. Some people, some companies, and some decision makers in particular have known exactly what priceless values they are sacrificing to continue making unimaginable amounts of money."*

January 25, 2019, WEF lunch panel:[223]

> *"Some people say that the climate crisis is something that we will have created. But that is not true. Because if everyone is guilty then no one is to blame. And someone is to blame. Some people, some companies, some decision-makers in particular, have known exactly what priceless values they have been sacrificing to continue making unimaginable amounts of money. And I think many of you here today belong to that group of people."*

This was not lost on the WEF organizers, whom, in a concerted effort with Greenpeace[224] and Extinction Rebellion,[225] were already sharing the Swedish ecommercial[226] within the WEF event and on social media – prior to the Salesforce lunch panel where Thunberg would cite the passages for media. The at-

220 "We work with individuals and organizations that are about the issues we face as human beings and meet our partnership guidelines. We offer our platform to scientists, environmentalists, activists, and any individual, group or organization including political candidates that meet these guidelines. **Uphill Media, is the continuation of Bernie2016 TV and Political Revolution TV.** We are 501(c)(3)3 non profit independent media network focused on informing the electorate through engagement on the Internet. Learn more @ http://UphillMedia.org. Read and share the Democratic Party of Oregon 2018 Platform. https://www.dpoplatform.org/" [Source: YouTube]

221 "Some people say that we are not doing enough to fight climate change. But that is not true. Because to "not do enough" you have to do something. And the truth is we are basically not doing anything. Yes, some people are doing more than they can, but they are too few or too far away from power to make a difference today. Some people say that the climate crisis is something that we all have created. But that is just another convenient lie. Because if everyone is guilty then no one is to blame. And someone is to blame. Some people, some companies, and some decision makers in particular [has][sic] known exactly what priceless values they are sacrificing to continue making unimaginable amounts of money. I ask you to stand o the right side of history. I ask you to pledge to do everything in your power to push your own business or government in line with a 1.5 degree world. Will you pledge to do that? Will you pledge to join me, and the people all around the world in doing whatever it takes. [Screen: #whateverittakes]

222 https://www.youtube.com/watch?v=Bdr4KZTujL8&feature=youtu.be&t=26

223 https://youtu.be/ScgUSdZNKxg

224 https://twitter.com/Greenpeace/status/1087768409733885952

225 https://youtu.be/5Fo69sPq_Og

226 https://twitter.com/wef/status/1087956623358914560

tempt by the media, and forces at play, to frame the speech as spontaneous, regardless if it was deliberate or not, evokes a layer of child-like authenticity by the messenger, if not the message itself. In spite of the motive, this is disingenuous to say the least.

This compounds with other earmarks of a well-orchestrated media campaign.

On December 15, 2018, Thunberg was thrust into international stardom following a speech at the COP24 in Katowice, Poland, that was published[227] on December 15, 2018 by Connect4Climate (a global partnership program under the World Bank) and other outlets. The video quickly went viral. The speech, as described by Quartz (December 15, 2018)[228] is representative of how global media framed the event to the public:

> *"Fifteen-year-old Swedish climate activist Greta Thunberg minced no words at the COP24 climate talks in Katowice, Poland this week. Speaking to the assembled countries Wednesday, at the most important climate negotiating meeting since the Paris talks in 2015... In a speech lasting under five minutes, Thunberg castigated leaders at the talks for decades of inaction and too-small steps in the face of climate crisis"*

Yet, a poor editing job in a Swedish newsroom inadvertently revealed yet another inconvenient truth – there was almost no one[229] in the auditorium when Thunberg spoke.[230]

Such inconsistencies between the real intent of the World Economic Forum ["Globalization 4.0: Shaping a Global Architecture in the Age of the Fourth Industrial Revolution"] and the re-framing for public perception[231] are best captured in the images shared on social media (see following page).

This bit of social engineering is stunning in its blatancy. Like magic, the telling word "salesforce" and the phrase "The Fourth Industrial Revolution" no longer appear in the image.

Gone are the obvious contradictions between the unprecedented magnitude of precious Earth metals including coltan and cobalt – a key requirement for the "fourth industrial revolution", which the mining of has decimated the chimp population Goodall claims to advocate for.[232]

227 https://youtu.be/VFkQSGyeCWg
228 https://qz.com/1497005/greta-thunberg-15-blasts-world-leaders-for-immaturity-at-cop24/
229 https://henrikalexandersson.blogspot.com/2018/12/klimat-greta-has-left-building.html
230 Video: Greta Thunbergs tal i Katowice enligt SvT Morgonstudion [Running time: 1m:15s] https://youtu.be/v2O7--voJ_g
231 https://www.facebook.com/567337650286414/photos/a.567343490285830/823735447979965/
232 [Jane Goodall Institute: "Many of the metals and minerals used in these technologies are extracted from threatened chimpanzee habitats across the Congo Basin. Control over these resources has also fueled conflict among people

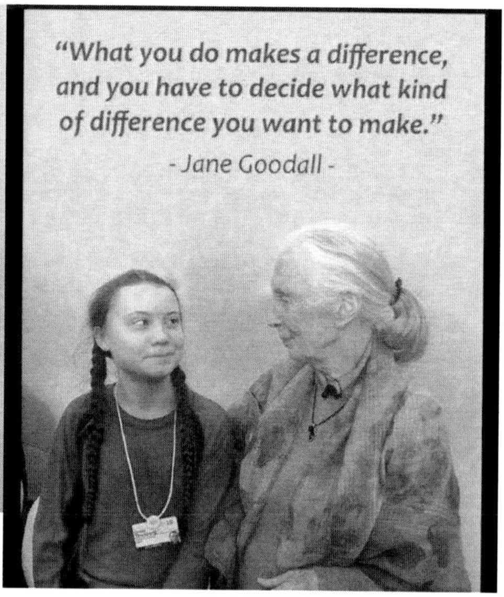


Such is the primary role of the non-profit industrial complex.

— conflict that has resulted in the deaths of more than five million people."]
http://www.janegoodall.org.nz/jgi-nz-campaigns/sustainable-selves/im:424/

## THE CLIMATE MOBILIZATION

> *"We launched at the People's Climate March in 2014 as the first group organizing for a WWII-scale climate response, an idea that had emerged as a hidden consensus among climate experts."*[233]

Here, we have an NGO that would very much appreciate Thunberg's sober and "flat" (CNN) delivery style. The Climate Mobilization.[234] Founded in 2014, at the People's Climate March, the founder and executive director of this US NGO is psychologist Margaret Klein Salamon.

The Climate Mobilization has one primary goal: "Our mission is to save civilization".[235] To do so, Salamon outlines a "wartime-style mobilization, akin to the American home front effort during World War II":

> *"The Climate Mobilization is a growing group of people who know that climate change threatens the collapse of civilization within this century. We believe, along with many well-respected scientists and environmental analysts, that the only way to preserve a climate that is safe, stable, and supportive of human civilization is to fight climate change with a World War II-scale mobilization."*

Salamon's strength, as a psychologist specializing in climate change, is exactly what Annex I states across the world are now embracing via the establishment of "nudge units". That is, the implementation and use of behavioural science for policy within government. ["Salamon earned her PhD in clinical psychology from Adelphi University and also holds a BA in social anthropology from Harvard. Via Climate Mobilization, Salamon applies her psychological and anthropological knowledge to solving climate change. She is the author of the blog The Climate Psychologist."][236]

The 2014 People's Climate March[237] was organized by the Global Call for Climate Action[238] (GCCA/TckTckTck),[239] Climate Nexus[240] ("Climate Nexus is dedicated to changing the conversation on climate change"), 350.org, USCAN[241]

233 https://www.theclimatemobilization.org/about-us
234 "The Climate Mobilization is a 501(c)(4) nonprofit and a sister organization of Climate Mobilization Project (501(c)(3). The Climate Mobilization supports the mission of Climate Mobilization Project (http://the-climate-mobilization-project.webflow.io/) through direct lobbying and political work." [Source: Climate Mobilization Website: https://www.theclimatemobilization.org/about-us]
235 https://www.linkedin.com/in/margaret-klein-salamon-a294a285/
236 http://www.theclimatepsychologist.com/
237 https://www.counterpunch.org/2014/07/30/netwar-in-the-big-apple/
238 http://www.wrongkindofgreen.org/2015/12/01/from-tcktcktck-to-air-france-to-earth-to-paris-havas-worldwide-continues-to-hypnotize/
239 https://twitter.com/tcktcktck?lang=en
240 https://climatenexus.org/
241 https://www.usclimatenetwork.org/

and Avaaz/Purpose.[242] At the helm of this NGO assemblage was the Rockefeller Brothers Fund working with the V.K. Rasmussen Foundation.

Additionally, Climate Nexus is a sponsored project of Rockefeller Philanthropy Advisors, a 501(c)3 organization.

> *"When the **Climate Mobilization was founded at the People's Climate March in 2014**, there was no climate group publically organizing around the need for WWII-scale emergency speed transition. Since then, we have worked to **establish an active 'emergency climate movement' wing of the broader climate movement**."* [243]

Eleven of The Climate Mobilization advisory board[244] members include:

• Betsy Taylor: president of Breakthrough Strategies & Solutions[245] consulting firm, co-founder of 1Sky (financed by the Clinton Global Initiative) that merged with 350.org (incubated by the Rockefeller Brothers Foundation) in 2011, advisory boards include 350.org and Ceres (350.org investment partner)

• Laura Dawn Murphy: former creative director[246] for MoveOn.Org [parent of Avaaz]

• Paul Gilding: former executive director of Greenpeace International, strategy advisor and founder of Changing Markets Foundation[247] ["The Changing Markets Foundation was formed to accelerate and scale up solutions to sustainability challenges by leveraging the power of markets." Clients include Unilever, BHP Billiton, DSM, Ford and DuPont.]

• Jamila Raqib: executive director of Albert Einstein Institute ["Raqib has worked with Dr. Gene Sharp, the world's foremost scholar on strategic nonviolent action since 2002. As the director of the Albert Einstein Institute she promotes the study and use of strategic nonviolent action."]

• Gus Speth: founder of the World Resources Institute and co-founder of the Natural Resources Defense Council

• Rev. Lennox Yearwood, Jr: president of the Hip Hop Caucus

• Richard Heinberg: senior fellow of the Post Carbon Institute

• Lise Van Susteren: American psychiatrist, named to the board of directors of Al Gore's The Climate Project in 2009, organized the first conference to focus

242 http://www.theartofannihilation.com/avaaz-the-globes-largest-most-powerful-behavioural-change-network-part-i/
243 https://www.theclimatemobilization.org/about-us
244 Full list: https://www.theclimatemobilization.org/advisory-board
245 https://www.breakthroughstrategiesandsolutions.com/key-subcontractors-and-collaborators
246 https://web.archive.org/web/20060418200842/http:/www.commondreams.org/headlines04/0704-01.htm
247 https://changingmarkets.org/about/

on the psychological impacts of climate change in 2009, co-authored "The Psychological Effects of Climate Change" published by the National Wildlife Federation where she serves on the board.

• Michael Mann: American climate scientist

• David Spratt and Philip Sutton: Spratt is the director of Breakthrough – National Centre for Climate Restoration.[248] [Breakthrough collaborates with the Club of Rome.] Spratt and Sutton co-authored the book Climate Code Red in 2008.

[The interlocking directorate of the non-profit industrial complex (NPIC) is extensive. As this series focuses on the marketing strategy itself, more than those constructing it, the above bios are purposely brief.]

The Climate Mobilization's foray into politics began with the "Mobilize California" (#MobilizeCA) campaign. Leading the effort with The Climate Mobilization was Naomi Klein and her Leap NGO (Leap L.A. Coalition), as well as a coal-ition of "like minded organizations".

The coalition, in partnership with Los Angeles City council member Paul Koretz, sought to initiate a "WWII-scale Climate Mobilization of L.A."[249]

By May 2018, the council voted unanimously "to explore the establishment of the country's first climate emergency mobilization department and set aside $500,000 in seed money toward the effort. In June 2018, Berkeley declared a climate emergency and committed to an Emergency Climate Mobilization and Just Transition to end greenhouse gas emissions and begin **drawing down the excess carbon** in the atmosphere as quickly as possible." Other cities would soon follow.[250]

Here it is critical to note the language: "**drawing down the excess carbon** in the atmosphere." Long gone are discussions on reducing or cutting carbon emissions. This is not coincidence. Rather it is again, strategic.

Two days prior to the 2014 People's Climate March, on September 19, 2014,[251] the article titled "The Founder of The Climate Mobilization Talks With Bridget Read About How Psychology—Not Science—May Be the Key to Ending America's Climate Denial" reported the following:

> *"In 356 words, The Climate Mobilization's Pledge to Mobilize calls on the United States government to commence a World War Two-*

248 https://www.breakthroughonline.org.au/
249 Video: Naomi Klein at launch of Los Angeles Climate Justice Mobilization 2025 Working Group [4m:59s]: https://youtu.be/QVvAwjzJ8I4
250 https://www.theclimatemobilization.org/about-us
251 https://www.guernicamag.com/margaret-klein-we-need-to-talk/

*scale mobilization to fight climate change:* ***to decrease our net greenhouse gas emissions 100% by 2025, to deploy a system of removing greenhouse gases from the atmosphere with wartime speed****, and to make reducing* ***net*** *GHGs 100% globally, with the same swiftness, a top political priority."*

The Climate Mobilization's influence within the NPIC is articulated in the following text outlining its groundwork with the US Democratic Party platform, as well as the Green New Deal:[252]

> *"The evidence of impact is clear, as* ***assertive wings of the Democratic Party[253] [5] as well as chapters of organizations such as 350.org and the Sierra Club adopt our prescriptions as core demands****. Congresswoman Alexandria Ocasio-Cortez signed our Pledge to Mobilize and has been outspoken[254] specifically for the need for emergency mobilization as part of the push for a House Select Committee on the Green New Deal."*[255] [256]

Today's re-designing of our Western subjugation is nothing different than what has been unveiled in the past. Whereas education, health, arts, and all sectors of society were shaped and financed by foundations and their capital largesse, today's "fourth industrial revolution" remains in the clutches of the ruling elite. This includes the 2014 People's Climate March – where The Climate Mobilization was born.

Extinction Rebellion (to be discussed in Act V) has three very broad demands,[257] the primary one being that governments must "enact legally binding policy measures to reduce carbon emissions to net zero by 2025" echoing the talking points[258] brought into the mainstream by the NPIC, the World Bank,[259] et al in 2014.

The term "net-zero emissions" does not mean zero emissions. Rather, it is the amount of emissions being put into the atmosphere being equal to the amount

252 http://www.wrongkindofgreen.org/2019/01/07/the-green-new-deal-has-an-afl-cio-problem/

253 "Our organizers successfully intervened in the 2016 Democratic primary elections, bringing WWII-scale Climate Mobilization into the discussion by successfully lobbying presidential candidate Bernie Sanders (I-VT) to embrace the idea. In July 2016, the need for WWII-scale mobilization was adopted into the Democratic Party Platform thanks to Climate Mobilization advisor and ally Russell Greene who was appointed to the platform committee by Bernie Sanders. This commitment was reaffirmed in August 2018 when Democratic National Committee passed a resolution calling for 'a national social and economic mobilization' to 'address the climate emergency' and 'restore a safe climate.'" https://www.theclimatemobilization.org/about-us

254 https://youtu.be/EYmvYS0DHA4

255 https://ocasio2018.com/gnd

256 https://www.theclimatemobilization.org/about-us

257 https://rebellion.earth/demands/

258 https://theelders.org/news/what-carbon-neutrality-—and-how-can-we-achieve-it-2050

259 http://www.worldbank.org/en/news/feature/2014/12/08/transforming-economy-achieve-zero-net-emissions

being "captured." Net-zero therefore, the requirement for massive investments into the technologies being developed and rolled out by Bill Gate's "Mission Innovation".[260] [For an example of this, one can read the much lauded "Off Fossil Fuels for a Better Future Act"[261] [Section 101–5 "We must significantly increase Federal R&D funding to develop and deploy the technologies needed for deep decarbonization in our economy. This was a proposal announced at the Paris Climate Accord with Bill Gates called Mission Innovation, which committed to double government investment in energy technology."][262][6] Here, it is vital to recognize that WEF and Mission Innovation formed a partnership[263] on June 1, 2017.

Net-zero is carbon capture and storage and a host of other technologies that promise business (and emissions) will continue – as usual. Consider the reality that while we are inundated with anti-pipeline protest coverage, there is zero opposition to the carbon capture projects that are slowly coming online, such as the Alberta Carbon Trunk Line[264] in Canada.

Indeed, the inconvenient "zero" [emissions] and "near zero" terminology in the 2014 AR5 Synthesis report was conveniently transformed to the "net zero" term we now see in the public realm, barely missing a beat.

But the real question is, how to save capitalism, which is described as being "now in free fall".[265]

With "capitalism in danger of falling apart" (a rare, cryptically honest quote from Al Gore), and years of stagnant global economic growth now in free fall, the Greta campaign must be understood for what it is. An elaborate distraction that has nothing to do with protecting the natural world, and everything to do with the manufacturing of consent. The required consent of the citizenry that will unlock the treasuries and public monies under the guise of climate protection.

But before we go further into what we can aptly describe as a politically correct – and unprecedented global bailout, we must look at how collective society can be successfully manipulated and manoeuvred, in order to sanction the release of the funds.

260 http://mission-innovation.net/2017/12/12/mi-launches-new-initiatives-at-one-planet-summit/
261 https://www.congress.gov/bill/115th-congress/house-bill/3671/text
262 Mission Innovation: "Mission Innovation (MI) is a global initiative of 23 countries and the European Commission (on behalf of the European Union). These 24 members have committed to seek to double public investment in clean energy RD&D (http://mission-innovation.net/our-work/tracking-progress/) and are engaging with the private sector (http://mission-innovation.net/our-work/private-sector-engagement/), fostering international collaboration (http://mission-innovation.net/our-work/innovation-challenges/) and celebrating innovators (http://mission-innovation.net/our-work/ideas-and-innovators/)." [Source: http://mission-innovation.net/our-members/]
263 http://mission-innovation.net/2018/07/31/collaboration-between-the-world-economic-forum-and-mission-innovation-next-steps-and-opportunities/
264 http://www.enhanceenergy.com/actl
265 [January 3, 2019]: http://www.globeinvestor.com/servlet/ArticleNews/story/GAM/20190103/RBIMBARLOWINDUSTRIAL

The very strategy to unlock the public purse – and thus save capitalism itself, is that of a climate emergency.

#climatestrike + #fridaysforfuture + #ExtinctionRebellion = #climateemergency

## LEADING THE PUBLIC INTO EMERGENCY MODE: "OUR HOUSE IN ON FIRE"

# Leading the Public into Emergency Mode

A New Strategy for the Climate Movement

[266]

266 https://www.theclimatemobilization.org/emergency-mode

*"If you don't know who Swedish teenager Greta Thunberg is, you can think of her as an international climate-change counterpart to Representative Alexandria Ocasio-Cortez. Like the rock-star congresswoman from New York, Thunberg is a charismatic young woman whose social-media savvy, moral clarity, and fearless speaking truth to power have inspired throngs of admirers to take to the streets for a better world and call out the politicians and CEOs who are standing in the way.*

*Thunberg claimed on her Twitter feed that there have been student strikes for climate on every continent except Antarctica—70,000 strikers in total last week. Meanwhile, the Swedish teenager continued to blast the elites in Davos, in flawless English. "Adults keep saying, 'We owe it to the young people to give them hope,'" she said. "But I don't want your hope.... I want you to act as you would in a crisis. I want you to act as if the house is on fire. Because it is." — The Kids Are Coming, January 28, 2019, The Nation*[267]

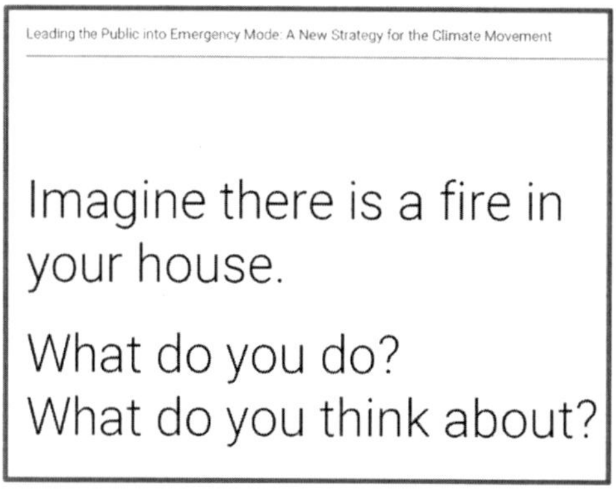
Leading the Public into Emergency Mode: A New Strategy for the Climate Movement

Imagine there is a fire in your house.

What do you do?
What do you think about?

In April 2016, The Climate Mobilization published the paper "Leading the Public into Emergency Mode: A New Strategy for the Climate Movement."[268]

The strategy document leads with:

**"Imagine there is a fire in your house.**

What do you do?

What do you think about?

You do whatever you can to try to put out the fire or exit the house. You make a plan about how you can put out the fire, or how you can best exit the house.

Our senses are heightened, you are focused like a laser, and you put your entire self into your actions.

You enter emergency mode."

– Leading the Public Into Emergency Mode, p. 2

267 https://www.thenation.com/article/greta-thunberg-climate-change-davos/
268 https://www.theclimatemobilization.org/emergency-mode

In the document, Salamon introduces "the concept of 'emergency mode' which is how individuals and groups function optimally during an existential or moral crisis — often achieving great feats through intensely focused motivation." She articulates that *"the goal of the climate movement must be to lead the public out of "normal" mode and into emergency mode".* [p. 2] [Emphasis in original.]

The emergency mode is enacted by the triggering of a switch.

> *"This has huge implications for the climate movement's communication style, advocacy, and strategy. Because emergency mode is contagious, the best strategy is for climate activists and organizations to go into emergency mode themselves, and communicate about the climate emergency, the need for emergency mobilization, and the fact that they are in emergency mode, as clearly and emphatically as possible." — Leading the Public into Emergency Mode: A New Strategy for the Climate Movement*[269]

And now, in 2019, we see how the strategy as laid out in the paper has now been deployed in real time, in real life.

> *"Since emotional ads create a deeper and more visceral impression on the memory centers of the brain, marketers are now measuring more cerebral responses to content using neurometrics tools like facial coding, implicit response testing, eye tracking, and magnetic resonance imaging (MRI)." — The Dangerous Power of Emotional Advertising, April 14, 2016*

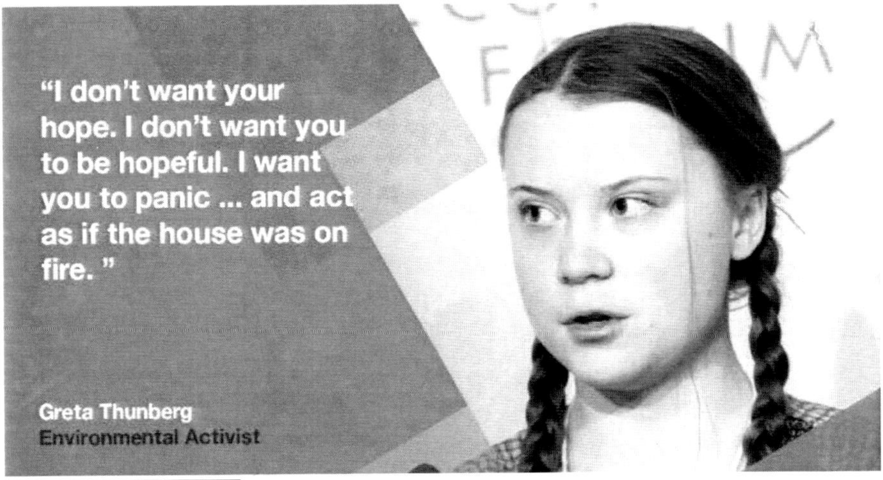


269 https://www.theclimatemobilization.org/emergency-mode

**Greta Thunberg**
@GretaThunberg
Follow

"Our house is on fire."
A part of my speech at the World Economic Forum today. Thank you for inviting me! #wef

11:17 AM - 25 Jan 2019

3,145 Retweets 9,882 Likes

210 3.1K 9.9K

**SDG2030**
@SDG2030
Follow

@wef Swedish teen #GretaThunberg slams #Davos elite over #climatechange hypocrisy str.sg/oLm

"Act as if your HOUSE 🏠 is on FIRE🔥"
@GretaThunberg

@deespeak @PattyArquette @biz @NaomiAKlein @AfrozShah1 @MikeHudema @AlexanderSoros @SwedenUN @EUatUN @swedense @n

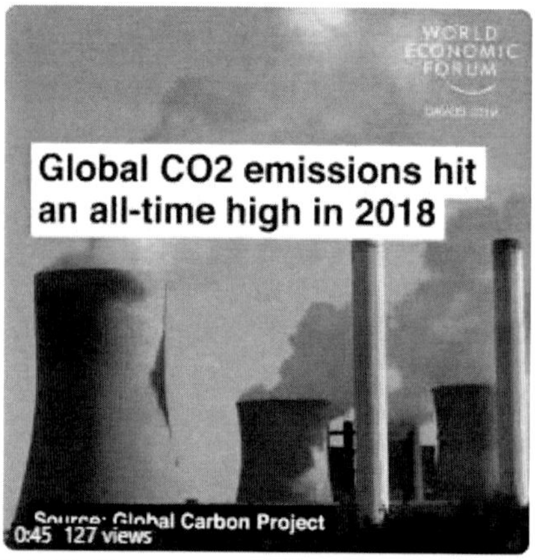


2:41 PM - 25 Jan 2019

17 Retweets 19 Likes

1 17 19

**World Economic Forum**
@wef
Follow

Time is running out. Read more:
wef.ch/2MuGnOk #environment #wef19

9:00 AM - 25 Jan 2019

991 Retweets 1,708 Likes

215 991 1.7K

**Guardian Environment**
@guardianeco
Follow

'Our house is on fire': Greta Thunberg, 16, urges leaders to act on climate

'Our house is on fire': Greta Thunberg, 16, urges leaders to act on climate
Swedish school strike activist demands economists tackle runaway global warming Read her Davos speech here
theguardian.com

10:17 AM - 25 Jan 2019

178 Retweets 333 Likes

8 178 333

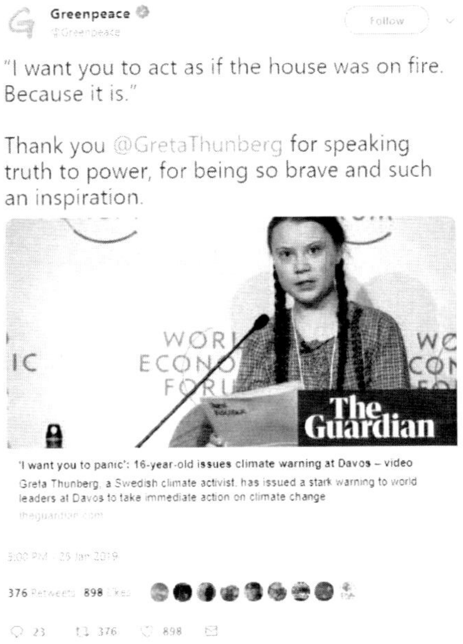


January 25, 2019,[270] 'Feel the fear': Climate change is now the talk of Davos, CNN:

> *"'Feel the fear' – The spirit of the event was reflected in two attendees with little in common: One is a former vice president of the United States; the other a 16-year-old Swedish schoolgirl.[271] What Al Gore and Greta Thunberg share is anger at corporate executives who aren't moving quickly enough to address climate change.* ***"I don't want you to be hopeful, I want you to panic, I want you to feel the fear I feel every day,"*** *Thunberg told attendees."*

270 https://www.cnn.com/2019/01/25/business/climate-change-davos/index.html
271 http://www.cnn.com/2019/01/25/europe/greta-thunberg-davos-world-economic-forum-intl/index.html

Support us →

The Guardian

News Opinion Sport Culture Lifestyle

▲ 'I want you to panic': 16-year-old issues climate warning at Davos - video

# 'Our house is on fire': Greta Thunberg, 16, urges leaders to act on climate

Greta Thunberg

Swedish school strike activist demands economists tackle runaway global warming. Read her Davos speech here

Fri 25 Jan 2019 14.57 GMT

Our house is on fire. I am here to say, our house is on fire.

## The Crux of the Strategy Document

The crux of the strategy document, Leading the Public into Emergency Mode: A New Strategy for the Climate Movement, is that citizens must first face, then accept that there is a life-threatening emergency in order to go into the necessary emergency mode. Once triggered, this enables the deployment of "a huge amount of resources toward solving the crisis" which would quickly become the clear, top priority for society [p. 4 & p. 5]. The more the climate movement provides "structures for people's engagement — clear directions and **support for people who are ready to tackle the climate emergency** — the more people will go into emergency mode." [p. 7]

Whereas budget restraint occurs in non-emergency mode, in emergency mode "all available /necessary resources are devoted to the emergency and, if necessary, **governments borrow heavily**." [p. 9]

> *"Economic mobilization is an emergency restructuring of a modern industrial economy, accomplished at rapid speed. It involves the vast majority of citizens, the utilization of a very high proportion of available resources, and impacts all areas of society. It is nothing less than a government-coordinated social and industrial revolution. Mobilization is what happens when an entire nation enters emergency mode, and the results can be truly staggering." [p. 8]*

Intentional or not, Salamon's paper weighs heavy with American exceptionalism. Notes of nationalism and cultural superiority waft throughout the document: "We also made huge advances in the sciences. The first computer was invented, as were blood transfusion and radar technology. The Manhattan Project successfully built the world's first atomic bomb in less than three years — a morally catastrophic but nonetheless stupendous feat of planning, cooperation and scientific ingenuity."

Reflecting the aforementioned observations, gone is the language to reduce or stop emissions. Consider the word "stop" does not appear once in the document, while the word "reduce" has one single entry: "If we only reduce the fossil fuel industry's stranglehold on politicians, the problem will solve itself." [p. 23]. Today's gently persuasive language is a mirror image of the language and demands drawn out in the strategy document: "restore a safe and stable climate", "draw down excess CO2" and "cool the planet".

> *"The way we respond to threats — by entering emergency mode or by remaining in normal mode — is highly contagious. Imagine the fire alarm goes off in an office building. How seriously should you take it? How do you know if it is a drill or a real fire?* ***Those questions will be predominantly answered by the actions and communications of the people around you, particularly people designated as leaders.*** *If they are chatting and taking their time exiting the building, you will assume that this is a drill. If people are moving with haste,* ***faces stern and focused, communicating with urgency and gravity,*** *you will assume there is real danger and exit as quickly as possible." [p. 14]*

The document acknowledges that the climate crisis is a "top threat to the global economy" (highlighted in red font in the original document, p. 21). What is not stated, yet understood, is the fact that the climate can also be exploited, to salvage the global economy. In essence, to save capitalism.

> *"We cannot be silent about the fact that emergency mobilization can only be coordinated by a "big" government that is granted the power to spend without limit to save as much life as possible." [p. 22]*

The document also outlines a cheerful camaraderie with the oppressors of the working class and those most marginalized:

> *"These pressure campaigns should escalate in degrees of assertiveness, all the way to disruptive protest. However, even in a protest, we must maintain an open, welcoming attitude. Thus, while we will need to be quite confrontational and unwavering,* ***we are not "against" our targets of protest****. We gain nothing from demonizing them. We need these leaders to do the right thing. The tone should not be primarily angry, but urgent and insistent.*
>
> *Rather,* ***the tone should be serious and patriotic****.* ***We are calling on America to lead the world in heroic, world-saving action!*** *Protests should involve elements of protestor sacrifice, such as risking arrest or hunger strike, to* ***generate empathy from the public****. Maintaining* ***strict non-violence is critical to winning widespread public support and is non-negotiable."*** *[p. 28]*

This document is astonishing in many ways. Not once does the author pause to reflect upon what specific societies and nations benefit from industrial civilization on our finite planet – and which ones are sacrificed for the same cause.

The said purpose of the strategy, is not the protection of what remains of the natural world, but rather, to save "organized civilization" [p. 2] and our "functioning global civilization" [p. 21]. The root word of civilization – is civil. And there is nothing civil about the industrial civilization we have built.

The savagery of our global economic system unleashed upon the biosphere, and both sentient and non-white human life, is certainly nothing to boast about – and certainly nothing to protect. It is the global capitalist economic system that upholds industrial civilization which must be deconstructed. It is both ironic and telling that even the societies who have benefited the most from industrialization, those in the West (and especially in North America), have never been more miserable. Today we witness an unprecedented crisis of mental illness and depression – with a massive percentage of society now dependent upon anti-depressant pharmaceuticals in order to function in a day-to-day existence.

Yet the most egregious aspect of this document, is that despite the references to Pearl Harbour, the atomic bomb and American war efforts of countless stripes, all cited as glowing examples of American ingenuity, NOWHERE is the militarism's impact on both climate and ecology mentioned. Consider the U.S. Department of Defense is the largest consumer of oil in the U.S. and the largest institutional consumer of oil in the world. With militarism's phenomenal contribution to global greenhouse gas emissions and environmental degradation – this omission is beyond the pale to say the least. This is the unspoken environmental racism and blatant eco-imperialism that hums beneath the foundational building blocks of the non-profit industrial complex.

> *"Here's the awful truth: even if every person, every automobile, and every factory suddenly emitted zero emissions, the earth would still be headed, head first and at full speed, toward total disaster for one major reason. The military produces enough greenhouse gases, by itself, to place the entire globe, with all its inhabitants large and small, in the most imminent danger of extinction." — The Green Zone: The Environmental Costs of Militarism[272] by Barry Sanders, May 1 2009 [The environmental of militarism podcast][273]*

272 https://www.akpress.org/greenzoneakpress.html
273 http://rpn.s3.amazonaws.com/s3fs-public/audio/rey-2010-10-21b.mp3

The power of conformity is a key aspect of social engineering. Its power is tragically often overlooked and grossly underestimated.

> ***"Thought Leaders and Leaders of Civil Society:*** *If people in the public eye, and in the public esteem go into emergency mode, they will significantly influence the broader public." — [p. 30]*

"The Race to Mobilize Is On, Cities around the globe are declaring Climate Emergency and committing to Climate Mobilization. Will your city join them?" The Climate Mobilization website

Of no surprise whatsoever is the fact, that since Extinction Rebellion's meteoric rise to stardom – in perfect symmetry with Thunberg, the group has announced a massive restructuring of the organization. The global expansion is being led by Salamon,[274] who launched the Extinction Rebellion US Twitter account on October 31, 2018 – the same day as the launch of Extinction Rebellion in the UK. The accompanying US website would launch on November 3, 2018[275] and the US Facebook group account would launch on November 4, 2018.[276] Between the official launch on October 31, 2018,[277] in the UK, to December 6, 2018, it grew to over 130 groups, across 22 countries.[278] By January 29, 2019, the Extinction Rebellion groups spanned across 50 countries. The Extinction Rebellion demands are not only complementary to The Climate Mobilization's emergency strategy, they are a mirror image of it with the slogan "tell the truth".

The September 20, 2018[279] Yale Climate Connections article "Climate Mobilization Plea: Cities Must Declare Emergency" references the "climate emergency language" gaining momentum in perfect stride with a cohesion of intersecting campaigns: the Thunberg campaign, the Extinction Rebellion protests, the Green New Deal, the general climate strikes, and the Fridays For Future youth climate strikes.

> *"Sanders, an independent who caucuses with the Democrats and ran for the Democratic nomination, isn't the only politician drawing parallels between climate change and fascist aggression. New York Democrat Alexandria Ocasio-Cortez, who has been hailed as an up-and-coming progressive champion, has spoken[280] about the need for a World War II-style commitment to fighting global warming. The Democratic Party in 2016 included similar language[281] in its official platform.*
>
> *The injection of this messaging into American political discourse can be traced in part to The Climate Mobilization,[282] a largely volunteer-run nonprofit founded in 2014."*

274 https://theenergymix.com/2018/11/26/extinction-rebellion-goes-global-with-call-for-net-zero-emission-by-2025/
275 https://twitter.com/Shwaydogg/status/1058693272300855296
276 https://www.facebook.com/ExtinctionRebellionUS/photos/a.944345139090589/944345672423899/?type=3&theater
277 https://www.theguardian.com/environment/2018/oct/26/facts-about-our-ecological-crisis-are-incontrovertible-we-must-take-action
278 December 6, 2018, "Margaret Klein Salamon talks to XR founders": https://www.youtube.com/watch?v=8AUFeT_QWwA
279 https://www.yaleclimateconnections.org/2018/09/climate-mobilization-plea-cities-must-declare-emergency/
280 https://qz.com/1316082/alexandria-ocasio-cortezs-green-new-deal-could-make-the-us-a-climate-change-leader/
281 https://www.theclimatemobilization.org/blog/2018/9/4/dnc-passes-climate-emergency-mobilization-resolution
282 https://www.theclimatemobilization.org/

August 15, 2016: "We're under attack from climate change—and our only hope is to mobilize like we did in WWII", by 350.org founder Bill McKibben. Illustration by Andrew Colin Beck. [Source: 350.org]

*"I assume that many activists will continue to be drawn to fossil fuel infrastructure protests. I recommend to them that they work as hard as possible to communicate the way forward (emergency mobilization off fossil fuels and carbon intensive agriculture, plus carbon drawdown to cool the earth back to a safe level) as much as possible in their verbal and non-verbal communications.* ***This can be as simple as wearing Rosie the Riveter bandanas while protesting, displaying a banner demanding WWII-scale climate mobilization to restore a safe climate, and including the demand for net zero emissions by 2025, plus large-scale drawdown, in press releases and web materials.****"*
*— April, 2016, Leading the Public into Emergency Mode: A New Strategy for the Climate Movement, April 2016 [p. 30]*

## A CLIMATE OF FEAR: CAPITALISM IS NOW IN FREE FALL

> *"Capitalism is in crisis, says World Economic Forum founder Klaus Schwab." —January 17, 2017,[283] Deutsche Welle*

Leading up to the January 2019 Davos gathering, a top Wall Street economist warned investors that they face a tough road ahead with global economic growth 'now in free fall'. The current headlines read like Orson Welle's economic version of "War of the Worlds".

January 3, 2019,[284] The Globe and Mail, "Global economic growth 'now in free fall':

> *"Merrill Lynch strategist Ajay Singh Kapur recently wrote that **"global [economic] growth is now in a broad, deep and persistent slowdown," creating market conditions that, I believe, will make life treacherous for commodity sectors and beyond..."***

> *"Since August, 2017, growth in manufacturing activity has been decelerating rapidly, dragging metal prices with them."*

January 15, 2019:[285]

> ***"Global economic growth is slowing**, including in Canada, according to new data from the Organization for Economic Co-Operation and Development (OECD)"*

January 21, 2019:[286]

> *IMF, CEOs Warn of Slowing World Economy on Eve of Davos Summit: "Corporate executives joined the International Monetary Fund in warning the global economy is slowing faster than expected, establishing a downbeat tone for this week's annual meeting of the World Economic Forum."*

January 21, 2019:[287]

> *"China's 6.6% growth in 2018 is its slowest in nearly 3 decades..."*

283 https://www.dw.com/en/capitalism-is-in-crisis/av-37155604
284 http://www.globeinvestor.com/servlet/ArticleNews/story/GAM/20190103/RBIMBARLOWINDUSTRIAL
285 https://www.baystreet.ca/globalmarkets/2247/Global-Economic-Growth-Is-Slowing-OECD-Report
286 https://www.bloomberg.com/news/articles/2019-01-21/imf-ceos-warn-of-slowing-world-economy-on-eve-of-davos-summit
287 https://www.wsj.com/articles/china-annual-economic-growth-rate-is-slowest-since-1990-11548037761

February 1, 2019:[288]

*"World's Largest Pension Fund Loses $136 Billion in Three Months"*

## TO THE RESCUE: A POLITICALLY CORRECT BAILOUT - THE CLIMATE FINANCE PARTNERSHIP

*"UNLOCKING THE INCLUSIVE GROWTH STORY OF THE 21ST CENTURY – Accelerating Climate Action in Urgent Times – This is our 'use it or lose it' moment. Investing the US$90 trillion to build the right infrastructure now will deliver a new era of economic growth. Investing it wisely will help drive innovation, deliver public health benefits, create a host of new jobs and go a long way to tackling the risks of runaway climate change. Getting it wrong, on the other hand, will lock us into a high-polluting, low productivity, and deeply unequal future." — The New Climate Economy[289] website, Executive Summary[290]*

Following the September 8, 2018 Rise for Climate[291] mobilization (a follow-up to the People's Climate March 2014, having been re-branded to the People's Climate Movement in 2017), the single goal behind the accelerating climate emergency language was finally unveiled at the September 26, 2018 One Planet Summit[292] in New York:

*"Efforts to blend capital in order to engage and mobilize large-scale institutional capital toward climate solutions took a notable step forward on September 26 at the One Planet Summit in New York, when French President Emmanuel Macron and BlackRock's Larry Fink announced the* ***Climate Finance Partnership (CFP).*** *The CFP consists of a unique combination of philanthropies, governments, institutional investors, and a leading global asset manager. The parties, including* ***BlackRock, the Governments of France and Germany, and the Hewlett, Grantham, and IKEA foundations****, have committed to work together to finalize the design and structure of what we anticipate will be a flagship*

288 https://www.bloomberg.com/news/articles/2019-02-01/world-s-biggest-pension-fund-reports-record-136-billion-loss
289 http://newclimateeconomy.net/about/members-global-commission/
290 https://newclimateeconomy.report/
291 https://350.org/press-release/rise-for-climate-september-8th/
292 https://www.un.org/sustainabledevelopment/blog/2018/09/one-planet-summit/

*blended capital investment vehicle* ***by the end of the first quarter, 2019.***"

Grantham Institute

**Grantham Imperial**
@Grantham_IC

Follow

"I want you to act as you would in a crisis. I want you to act as if our house is on fire. Because it is." @GretaThunberg urges leaders at #WEF2019 #Davos to act on #climatechange | Read in full via @guardianeco theguardian.com/environment/20 ...

10:56 AM - 25 Jan 2019

September 26, 2018,[293] "Governments and Philanthropies Announce Groundbreaking Partnership with BlackRock to Mobilize and Deploy Climate Finance at Scale":

> *"France, Germany, the Hewlett, Grantham and IKEA foundations, and asset manager BlackRock today announced the* ***Climate Finance Partnership*** *at the One Planet Summit in New York. The*

293 https://europeanclimate.org/governments-and-philanthropies-announce-ground-breaking-partnership-with-blackrock-to-mobilize-and-deploy-climate-finance-at-scale/

*Climate Finance Partnership is an* ***unprecedented cooperation between philanthropies, governments and private investors****, which have* ***committed to jointly developing an investment vehicle*** *that will aim to invest in* ***climate infrastructure in emerging markets****."*

The two institutions identified as the media contacts for the above unprecedented announcement, are the European Climate Foundation and the aforementioned Climate Nexus[294] – a lead organizer for the 2014 People's Climate March.[295]

On November 8, 2018, the article "The Climate Finance Partnership:[296] Mobilizing Institutional Capital to Address the Climate Opportunity" discloses where the money will come from for the "fourth industrial revolution", sold to the public under the guise of sustainability:

*"Nowhere is the investment gap[297] between what is needed and what is currently flowing greater and more urgent, or the opportunities more significant, than in the* ***world's developing and emerging markets. These economies are generally characterized by growing populations, rapidly increasing energy demand, and extraordinary infrastructure investment needs.[298]*** *But they also tend to have less developed capital markets and* ***higher political and regulatory risk*** *than their developed country counterparts. Institutional investors may therefore be partially forgiven for moving cautiously, even in the face of compelling long-term economic and demographic drivers.*

*A detailed analysis[299] by the World Bank found that while* ***$100 trillion is held by pension funds*** *and other institutional investors, these same investors allocated less than $2 trillion over a 25 year period into infrastructure investment in emerging markets. And the fraction of that investment that could be considered green, clean, or climate-friendly was negligible.*

294 https://climatenexus.org/
295 https://youtu.be/KT0rifzhbd4
296 https://www.atlanticcouncil.org/blogs/energysource/the-climate-finance-partnership-mobilizing-institutional-capital-to-address-the-climate-opportunity
297 http://gggi.org/wp-content/uploads/2017/03/Mind-the-Gap_web.pdf
298 https://www.outlook.gihub.org/
299 https://library.pppknowledgelab.org/documents/5450?ref_site=kl

*So, what can be done? Whether you choose to look through the lens of unprecedented challenge or unprecedented opportunity,* ***there is violent agreement that institutional capital needs to be "unlocked"*** *(a favorite word on the climate conference circuit) and* ***mobilized quickly and at scale****."*

It is here that the accelerating "demand" for countries to align with the Paris Agreement becomes clear: "The Paris Agreement **requires** us to align finance flows in support for a low carbon and climate resilient development." Note the word "requires". What was considered non-binding one moment, conveniently becomes binding when it involves opening up the treasuries and pension plans to our corporate overlords.

No risk, all reward. The double speak of Wall Street is deliberately opaque. Yet, in layman's terms, these are simply high-finance words to say there is less risk in using someone else's money other than your own:

*"Blended finance, or the strategic deployment of public or other concessional capital to de-risk institutional capital investment, offers one compelling answer." Recently, the Blended Finance Task Force, a broad-based interdisciplinary effort, finalized a comprehensive report*[300] *identifying key barriers to large-scale institutional capital mobilization toward the Sustainable Development Goals, and then subsequently designed a detailed Action Program*[301] *to address these barriers."* [302]

The **Blended Finance Taskforce** comprises of fifty icons of finance including HSBC, Credit Suisse, Citi, JP Morgan Chase, USAID, WEF–Sustainable Development Investment Partnership[303] (SDIP), World Bank, Investec, MacArthur Foundation, Allianz, EBRD, ClimateWorks (founded by the Hewlett, Packard, and McKnight foundations) and the Rockefeller Foundation.[304]

*"The partnership, coordinated by the* ***Task Force on Philanthropic Innovation*** *and the Aligned Intermediary, an investment advisory group,* ***was designed and structured specifically to use a layer of government and philanthropic capital*** *to max-*

300 http://s3.amazonaws.com/aws-bsdc/BFT_BetterFinance_final_01192018.pdf#asset:614:url
301 https://www.blendedfinance.earth/action-programme-placeholder/
302 https://www.atlanticcouncil.org/blogs/energysource/the-climate-finance-partnership-mobilizing-institutional-capital-to-address-the-climate-opportunity
303 http://sdiponline.org/updated_members-and-partners/
304 [Full list: https://www.blendedfinance.earth/steering-committee/]

*imize private capital mobilization toward climate-related sectors in emerging markets."* [305]

And here again, is where more stark reality is faintly disclosed:

> *"Doing so in partnership with the world's largest manager and its set of world-class institutional investor clients should send an important signal to fund managers and institutional investors alike that **there are profits to be had in sectors and geographies where this capital has not historically deployed**...*
>
> *"The partnership will seek to make investments in a targeted set of sectors including renewable energy, energy efficiency, energy storage, and low-carbon and electrified transportation, **across three regions including Latin America, Asia, and Africa**".*

Today's climate emergency mobilization must be recognized for what it is: a strategically orchestrated campaign financed and managed by the world's most powerful institutions – for the preservation of capitalism and global economic growth. This is the launch of a new growth industry in the Global South coupled with the creation of new and untapped markets. Leading up to this precipice, The B Team,[306] the Open Society Foundation,[307] Oxfam,[308] and many others that serve as the human face of capitalism have moved their offices to or set up new divisions in both Africa and Latin America.

Also of threat, to Western imperialism, is a burgeoning China. And to be clear – there will be no "fourth industrial revolution" for the Western ruling class – without uninterrupted and perpetual access to Africa's bounty of rare earth minerals and metals:

> *"While significant progress has been made on Africa's political and economic transformation, the continent continues to face significant challenges. Geopolitically, new economic alliances are altering traditional relationships and spheres of influence."* [309]

The sycophantic NGOs – in servitude, indeed on the very same team as their corporate benefactors, created a literal, albeit virtual firestorm (encapsulated in the mantra "our house is on fire") – in order to instigate a "climate revolu-

305 https://www.atlanticcouncil.org/blogs/energysource/the-climate-finance-partnership-mobilizing-institutional-capital-to-address-the-climate-opportunity
306 https://www.virgin.com/virgin-unite/introducing-b-team-eastern-africa
307 https://uk.tetris-db.com/projects/innovative-project-historical-patrimony/
308 https://qz.com/africa/737094/oxfam-is-moving-its-international-headquarters-to-nairobi-where-it-might-not-be-welcome/
309 [Source: WEF 2019: https://www.weforum.org/events/world-economic-forum-on-africa]

tion". The collective energy of the West stemming from a growing societal discontent, is being captured and utilized – transcending into a new weapon of choice that will aid the further colonization of the Global South. A climate revolution in name only, this said emergency has nothing to do with the protection of our Earth – or climate – and never will have. Rather, it has everything to do with saving, protecting and expanding the capitalist economy – at the expense of our already decimated planet. And nothing more than that. This oncoming new onslaught of environmental devastation and plunder – in the name of climate revolution – will make all of modern man's historical violence against nature, up to this point – seem like childish prattle.

Yet none of this should come as a surprise. As the oligarchs financed, shaped and largely managed the climate movement – it's only natural that they alone benefit from it. The power-elites repackaged our oppression as revolution and sold it back to us. By exploiting the innocent youth, which in turn exploited our emotions and fears as a collective populace, we devoured it. And soon, young Greta, and all the youth they have exploited, will be thrown under the bus. It's all par for the course under capitalism.

# ACT V

## THE GREEN NEW DEAL IS THE TROJAN HORSE FOR THE FINANCIALIZATION OF NATURE

### A GREEN NEW DEAL – FOR MOBILIZATION

November 12, 2018, A New Global Architecture: Børge Brende [Far left of panel], President, Member of the Managing Board, World Economic Forum and panel. "Shaping a New Global Architecture" session at the World Economic Forum, Annual Meeting of the Global Future Councils 2018. Copyright by World Economic Forum / Benedikt von Loebell
310

310 A New Global Architecture, November 12, 2018: Børge Brende, President; Member of the Managing Board, World Economic Forum and panel, Maxim Oreshkin, Minister of Economic Development of the Russian Federation; Young Global Leader, Helen E. Clark, Prime Minister of New Zealand (1999 – 2008), New Zealand, Roland Paris, University of Ottawa, Canada, Jean-David Levitte, Adviser, France; Former Ambassador of France to the UN and United States Hilary Cottam, Author and Entrepreneur, Centre for the Fourth Social Revolution; Young

March 10, 2014:[311]

> *"...the divestment campaign will result (succeed) in a colossal injection of money shifting over to the very portfolios heavily invested in, thus dependent upon, the intense commodification and privatization of Earth's last remaining forests, (via REDD, environmental "markets" and the like). This tour de force will be executed with cunning precision under the guise of environmental stewardship and "internalizing negative externalities through appropriate pricing." Thus, ironically (if in appearances only), the greatest surge in the ultimate corporate capture of Earth's final remaining resources is being led, and will be accomplished, by the very environmentalists and environmental groups that claim to oppose such corporate domination and capture." — McKibben's Divestment Tour – Brought to You by Wall Street [Part II of an Investigative Report, The "Climate Wealth" Opportunists]*

The "New Deal" of the 1930s has always been a point of pride in the American psyche since its implementation by Franklin Delano Roosevelt during his four terms in office after the Great Depression. Since that time, various people and programs have attempted to appropriate this term in furtherance of diverse platforms as a means to portray the concept as beneficial to a populace. In that regard, a fairly recent phrase that has been borrowed from this terminology is the "Green New Deal". This term first surfaced during 2007 when referenced by the NY Times columnist Thomas L. Friedman and was then used by London accountant Richard Murphy to describe a full-scale change in our economy to an environmentally sound capitalist system. As the term has never been fully embraced by the establishment, it still resided right below the surface of mainstream economic discourse among many people, as it serves as a potential improvement within the current economic system. Only recently though, in 2019, has the "Green New Deal" reached apoplectic proportions as far as its usage and reached a fevered pitch by those who are touting its ability to shift the paradigm from fossil fuels to a panacea of "green technologies" in the near future.

Prior to 2018, the term had become most recognized and associated with the Green Party[312] as part and parcel of its platform. By June 2018, however, traces of how this would soon serve to be the vehicle that would launch

Global Leader during the Session "Shaping a New Global Architecture" at the World Economic Forum, Annual Meeting of the Global Future Councils 2018. Copyright by World Economic Forum / Benedikt von Loebell

311 http://www.theartofannihilation.com/350-orgs-friends-on-wall-street-the-climate-wealth-opportunists-part-ii-of-an-investigative-report/

312 https://blackagendareport.com/raising-bar-green-new-deal

Alexandria Ocasio-Cortez into the stratosphere of a superstar would start to surface.

On June 27, 2018,[313] Democracy Now, a popular mouthpiece for the halls of power in the domestic pseudo-left movements, reported the following:

> *"In a stunning upset and the biggest surprise of the primary season this year, 28-year-old Democratic Socialist Alexandria Ocasio-Cortez beat 10-term incumbent Representative Joe Crowley in New York in Tuesday's Democratic primary. Crowley is the fourth-ranking Democrat in the House, and he'd outraised Ocasio-Cortez by a 10-to-1 margin. Crowley was widely viewed as a possible future House speaker. Yet Ocasio-Cortez defeated Crowley after running a progressive grassroots campaign advocating for "Medicare for All" and the abolition of ICE, the Immigration and Customs Enforcement agency."*

Following her victory on June 26, 2018, Ocasio-Cortez would acknowledge that the only reason she ran for the seat was at the bequest of the Justice Democrats[314] and Brand New Congress[315] who had approached her a year and a half earlier, in 2016.[316]

The Young Turks: "Last, two things real quick. You're among the first Just Democrat candidates ever in history. Umm, how much of a, of a help was that organization to you?

Alexandria Ocasio-Cortez: It was enormously important. I wouldn't be running if it wasn't for the support of Justice Democrats and Brand New Congress. Umm, in fact it was it was these organizations, it was JD and it was Brand New Congress as well, that both, that asked me to run in the first place. They're the ones that called me a year and a half ago after I left Standing Rock and said 'hey would you be willing to run for Congress?' So I wouldn't be here, um, and I wouldn't have run if it wasn't [for them]."

Most of the people involved[317] in founding the Justice Democrats (launched in January 2017) and Brand New Congress (founded in 2016) came from the aftermath of the Bernie 2016 campaign. As an example, Saikat Chakrabarti, co-founder and former executive director of Justice Democrats, as well as a co-founder of Brand New Congress, served as the campaign chair during Alexandria Ocasio-Cortez's 2018 campaign. Today, Chakrabarti serves as Ocasio-

313 https://youtu.be/8SKwelcurCM
314 https://www.justicedemocrats.com/
315 https://brandnewcongress.org/
316 [Video interview, June 27, 2018, 9m:42s in]: https://youtu.be/X7SIHsPWYEs
317 https://campaignforamericasfuture.org/signer/corbin-trent/

Cortez's chief of staff.[318] Prior to co-founding Justice Democrats and Brand New Congress, Chakrabarti was the director of organising technology for the Bernie 2016 Campaign.

Our Revolution, a political organization launched by Bernie Sanders[319] in 2016,[320] [touched upon in ACT III of this series] also endorsed Ocasio-Cortez. On January 23, 2017,[321] it was reported that Justice Democrats would partner with Brand New Congress.

October 26, 2018: Brand New Congress, Green New Deal

One name that sparks curiosity is Zack Exley.[322] In addition to serving as current advisor to US congresswoman Alexandria Ocasio-Cortez, Exley is a co-founder of both Justice Democrats and Brand New Congress. Previously, he served as the senior advisor to the Bernie 2016 campaign and the organizing director for MoveOn. Exley, Open Society Fellow,[323] is co-founder of the New Consensus[324] public relations and communications firm and the ascribed "policy arm of Justice Democrats."[325] New Consensus,[326] co-author of The Green New Deal document with the Sunrise Movement and the Justice Democrats, is identified[327] by Think Progress as "the muscle supporting Green New Deal efforts".

Exley, co-author of "Rules for Revolutionaries: How Big Organizing Can Change Everything", was also co-founder of the New Organizing Institute (launched in 2005) which recruited, trained and supported US po-

318 https://www.thequint.com/neon/social-buzz/alexandria-ocasio-cortez-saikat-chakrabarti-chief-of-staff
319 https://vtdigger.org/2018/07/29/sanders-institute-little-show-first-year-500k/
320 https://www.usatoday.com/story/news/politics/elections/2016/07/15/bernie-sanders-progressive-message/87073052/
321 https://mic.com/articles/166390/cenk-ugyur-bernie-sanders-staffers-team-up-to-take-over-the-democratic-party#.dlnuE8PQ6
322 https://www.linkedin.com/in/zackexley/
323 https://www.youtube.com/watch?v=Ps7sYvjFQQ8
324 https://newconsensus.com/people/
325 https://www.vox.com/energy-and-environment/2018/12/21/18144138/green-new-deal-alexandria-ocasio-cortez
326 https://twitter.com/newconsensus/following
327 https://thinkprogress.org/green-new-deal-alexandria-ocasio-cortez-democrats-95cb356e94ca/

litical candidates. New Organizing Institute, funded by Open Society Foundations[328] and the Ford Foundation among others, partnered with MoveOn.org (co-founder of both Avaaz and the New Organizing Institute) and several other NGOs in 2011 before the institute was dissolved[329] in 2015.

It is worth noting that Avaaz first polled its members on a Green New Deal in 2009.

One day after Ocasio-Cortez won the Democratic nomination for her congressional district on June 27, 2018,[330] a Green New Deal led by Ocasio-Cortez was highlighted by Grist in which they referenced an email interview between HuffPost and Ocasio-Cortez the week prior:

> *"What sets Ocasio-Cortez's proposal apart is her plan to meet the target by implementing what she called a "Green New Deal," a federal plan to spur "**the investment of trillions of dollars** and the creation of millions of high-wage jobs."*
>
> *Though the slogan harks back to President Franklin D. Roosevelt's 1930s New Deal program of infrastructure spending and labor reforms, she compared the program **she envisions to the tens of billions of dollars spent on armaments manufacturing and the rebuilding of Europe after World War II**."*
>
> *'The Green New Deal we are proposing will be similar in scale to the mobilization efforts seen in World War II or the Marshall Plan,' she told HuffPost by email last week. "We must again invest in the development, manufacturing, deployment, and distribution of energy, but this time green energy."*

On June 30, 2018, Grist would reference the Green New Deal as proposed by Ocasio-Cortez again:

> *"The Green New Deal we are proposing will be similar in scale to the mobilization efforts seen in World War II or the Marshall Plan', she said by email. "It will require the investment of trillions of dollars and the creation of millions of high-wage jobs. We must again invest in the development, manufacturing, deployment, and distribution of energy but this time green energy."*

328 https://www.opensocietyfoundations.org/about/programs/us-programs/grantees/new-organizing-institute-education-fund
329 https://www.buzzfeednews.com/article/evanmcsan/new-organizing-institute-implodes#.wf5bWyK7d
330 https://www.huffingtonpost.ca/entry/ocasio-cortez-climate-change_us_5b3307a5e4b0b5e692f25e18

Here we must pause for a moment to deconstruct the above. First, the above plan and language mirrors that in the strategy document "Leading the Public into Emergency Mode: A New Strategy for the Climate Movement" [laid out in ACT IV of this series] being led by organizations whose affiliations with the Democrats, the Sanders and Ocasio-Cortez campaigns are publicly disclosed. Second, we must recognize that behind large institutions and media outlets such as Grist, branded as both "left" and "progressive", are power structures subservient to capital. Grist CEO is Brady Walkinshaw. Prior to his role of CEO in 2017, Walkinshaw, a former US State representative, worked as a program officer at the Bill & Melinda Gates Foundation. Before his tenure at the Gates Foundation, Walkinshaw, a Fulbright scholar of the US State Department, worked as a special assistant to the World Bank. Within the Grist board of directors is 350.org founder, Bill McKibben – defacto foot soldier for Bernie Sanders and the Democrats in general.

# CLIMATE NEXUS: A GREEN NEW DEAL IS COMING

NEXUS HOT NEWS
by climatenexus

**Here It Comes:** Rep. Alexandria Ocasio-Cortez (D-NY) and Sen. Ed Markey (D-MA) will unveil a landmark resolution calling for a transition to renewable energy and the creation of thousands of new jobs today in Washington, DC. The highly-anticipated Green New Deal legislation follows months of protest and calls for an aggressive and just transition off fossil fuels from young activists in groups like the Sunrise Movement. Republicans are paying attention to the energy behind the movement: the Huffington Post reports that conservative politicians and witnesses called by the minority to testify showcased sharpened attacks on the Green New Deal. (GND: AP, The Guardian, Reuters, Axios, Bloomberg, Huffington Post. Activism: CNN. Conservative pushback: Huffington Post. Commentary: NPR, Alexandria Ocasio-Cortez interview, USA Today Q&A)

CLIMATE NEWS

On February 7, 2019, Climate Nexus (a sponsored project of Rockefeller Philanthropy Advisors)[331] announced via its "TOP STORIES" that a "Green New Deal is Coming":

> *"Here It Comes: Rep. Alexandria Ocasio-Cortez (D-NY) and Sen. Ed Markey (D-MA) will unveil a landmark resolution calling for a transition to renewable energy and the creation of thousands of new jobs today in Washington, DC. The highly-anticipated Green New Deal legislation follows months of protest and calls for an aggressive and just transition off fossil fuels from young activists in groups like the Sunrise Movement."*

331 "Climate Nexus, a sponsored project of Rockefeller Philanthropy Advisors, helps local, national, and international media recognize climate science and clean energy's role in addressing climate change. This is accomplished by building a broad network of influential, persuasive messengers, and creating a clear, compelling narrative about climate change and ways to address its impacts."

**Climate Nexus**
@ClimateNexus

Follow

Democrats' #GreenNewDeal wing takes shape amid wave of progressive #climate hawk wins buff.ly/2zy2M7B via @HuffPost @AlexCKaufman

10:27 PM - 7 Nov 2018

**5** Retweets **27** Likes

5 27

November 7, 2018, Twitter: Climate Nexus (a sponsored project of Rockefeller Philanthropy Advisors), Green New Deal

From 2013-2016, the MacArthur Foundation awarded Rockefeller Philanthropy Advisors ten million dollars for Climate Nexus.

The Blended Finance Taskforce[332] [see ACT IV of this series] comprises fifty icons of finance including the MacArthur and Rockefeller foundations.

As touched upon in Act IV of this series, the People's Climate March, which took place on September 21, 2014, was led and financed by the Rockefeller Foundation, Climate Nexus, 350.org,[333] Avaaz/Purpose,[334] Greenpeace,[335] US Climate Action Network (USCAN) and GCCA/TckTckTck[336] (founded by twenty NGOs with 350.org, Greenpeace, Avaaz and Oxfam[337] at the helm). In relation to the current set of circumstances, 350.org (incubated by the Rockefeller Foundation) would again serve to be an instrumental vehicle to propel the Green New Deal[338] as the catalyst to unlock the 100 trillion dollars required to unleash the "fourth industrial revolution". This project, of unparalleled magnitude, is the vehicle to save the failing global capitalist economic system and bring in the financialization of nature.

## GREEN NEW DEAL – DATA FOR PROGRESS

> *"A Green New Deal is **popular among American voters** and can mobilize them in 2018." — A Green New Deal Policy Report by Data for Progress, September, 2018[339] [Emphasis in original]*

350 ACTION

DATA FOR PROGRESS

Data for Progress website

332 https://www.blendedfinance.earth/steering-committee/
333 http://www.theartofannihilation.com/rockefellers-1sky-unveils-the-new-350-org-more-more-delusion/
334 http://www.theartofannihilation.com/avaaz-the-globes-largest-most-powerful-behavioural-change-network-part-i/
335 http://www.academia.edu/3880272/Greenpeace_International_Cites_Maximum_1C_UNAGGG_October_1_1997
336 http://www.theartofannihilation.com/category/articles-2013/the-most-important-cop-briefing-that-no-one-ever-heard-truth/
337 https://www.independent.co.uk/news/world/oxfam-sexual-misconduct-scandal-report-haiti-racism-bullying-colonial-behaviours-a8731831.html
338 http://www.wrongkindofgreen.org/2019/01/07/the-green-new-deal-has-an-afl-cio-problem/
339 https://www.dataforprogress.org/green-new-deal/

*"**Key Finding 7: The kids are alright** – Though some of the proposals we examine are currently unpopular nationally, that may change in the future. We find that four of the most radical proposals we analyzed are vastly more popular with younger voters than they are with the general public." — Data for Progress, Polling the Left Agenda*[340]

In July 2018, polling conducted by Data for Progress, a partner in the Green New Deal with the Sunrise Movement and 350.org, showed a whopping 41% of people under the age of 30 would support a candidate that campaigned on a jobs guarantee and clean energy. The support exhibited by this age bracket constituted approximately twice that of the group comprising people age 45 and above. ["Forty-eight percent of voting eligible adults said they would be more likely to support a candidate who was running on 100% renewable energy by 2030. Notably, this is significantly faster than even the most progressive legislation currently in Congress."] By targeting the youth, in addition to its 30-45 demographic, the promise of green jobs and clean energy were the clear winners.

*"In this case, at least, time could be a weapon for the Sunrise Movement. Earlier this year, the Pew Research Center projected that millennials were poised to overtake baby boomers as the largest adult generation in the U.S., as well as its biggest eligible voting bloc."* [341]

*"What year were you born? (Sunrise is building a movement led by young people; we ask for the year you were born so that we can help you find the best opportunities to engage. You can answer "prefer not to say" as well, but knowing this really helps us!)" — Sunrise Movement Website*

*"All electricity consumed in America must be generated by renewable sources, including solar, wind, hydro, geothermal, sustainable biomass, and renewable natural gas, as well as clean sources such as nuclear and remaining fossil fuel with carbon capture." — Green New Deal Policy Report*[342] *by Data for Progress, September, 2018 [p. 5]*

340 https://www.dataforprogress.org/polling-the-left-agenda/
341 https://www.eenews.net/stories/1060108439
342 https://www.dataforprogress.org/s/GreenNewDeal_Final_v2_12MB.pdf

September 6, 2018, Twitter: 350.org, Green New Deal, Data for Progress

For the Green New Deal's foray into the American consciousness, a new movement would be required. This would be the Sunrise Movement. A youth movement created under the direction of the Sierra Club from which it received a $50,000 grant. Par for the course of "youth grassroots activism" Sunrise already has a hefty budget and a full time staff: "In relation to other environmental groups, the Sunrise Movement is relatively small. Its officials said they have about 16 full-time staff and that they've raised about $1 million since its founding." [December 3, 2018][343]

Sunrise Movement is the rebranded[344] US Climate Plan (now defunct)[345] founded by Evan Weber[346] and Matt Lichtash.

Lichtash is a strategy and executive office specialist at the New York Power Authority. He is the founder of Carbon Capital.[347]

## 2013

**THE CLASS OF** 2013 is one year away from our Fifth Reunion and we're feeling the feels. Read on to see what we've been up to in 2017!

In March, **Evan Weber** was recognized by *Grist* as one of 50 emerging green leaders to watch for his work with U.S. Climate Plan, the organization he and **Matt Lichtash** started at Wesleyan. In April, U.S. Climate Plan re-branded as Sunrise, and is building a movement of young people to make climate action an urgent political priority, with an eye on a major intervention in the 2018 midterm elections.

WESLEYAN, ISSUE 2, 2017

343 https://www.eenews.net/stories/1060108439
344 https://www.pscp.tv/usclimateplan/1lDGLMWXjRLJm
345 http://usclimateplan.org/
346 https://thenextsystem.org/node/554
347 http://thecarboncapital.org/

In 2017, Weber was named by Grist as one of "50 emerging green leaders to watch for" citing his work with U.S. Climate Plan, the organization founded by he and Lichtash in 2013 under the direction of Michael Dorsey.

SustainUS alumni ["WE TRAIN YOUNG PEOPLE TO LEAD"][348] Dyanna Jaye[349] would be identified as one of the Sunrise Movement co-founders following the April 2017 rebrand, as would Varshini Prakash[350] and Sara Blazevic from the Fossil Fuel Divestment Student Network.

> *"Sunrise is a movement led by young people and young people will be prioritized for housing, travel support, and other needs, as people typically left out of the political process by our institutions. That being said, we welcome people of all ages to participate in Sunrise actions in different ways." — Sunrise website*

The president and executive director of the Sunrise Movement is Michael Dorsey. Having served eleven years on the Sierra Club national board, Dorsey is co-founder and principal of Around the Corner Capital—an energy advisory and impact finance platform. He serves as an advisor to ImpactPPA,[351] equity partner in the solar firm Univergy-CCC, co-founder and director of Univergy-CCC's India division (Univergy/ThinkGreen), and is a full member of the Club of Rome. His political background is extensive[352] having served under the US administrations of George H. W. Bush and Bill Clinton. He also served on Senator Barack Obama's energy and environment presidential campaign team.[353]

> *"We must end all emissions from fossil fuels. The full U.S. economy can and must run on a mix of energy that is either zero-emission or 100 percent carbon capture by mid-century* [*citation]."[354] — Green New Deal Policy Report[355] by Data for Progress, September, 2018 [p. 5]*

348 https://sustainus.org/
349 https://sustainus.org/people/dyanna-jaye/
350 https://issuu.com/uscan/docs/uscan_annual_report_2017_issuu
351 https://www.impactppa.com/
352 https://www.linkedin.com/in/profmkd/
353 "A former Dartmouth College professor, Dorsey is a serial organization builder & leader in for-profit, non-profit & governmental realms. In the for-profit arena, Dorsey co-founded and heads Around the Corner Capital—an energy advisory and impact finance platform. Thru Around the Corner he actively invests & advises several pools of private equity finance on renewable energy & related matters globally. Dr. Dorsey is an equity partner in the Spanish-Japanese solar firm: Univergy-CCC; and a co-founder of its India division: Univergy/ThinkGreen, based in Hyderabad.
In the non-profit arena Dr. Dorsey sits on many boards, including Food First & the Center for Environmental Health–the latter he co-created in 1997. Dorsey co-founded IslandsFirst.org. He served 11 years on the Sierra Club national board." [Source: https://www.linkedin.com/in/profmkd/]
354 https://www.pnnl.gov/main/publications/external/technical_reports/PNNL-26174.pdf
355 https://www.dataforprogress.org/s/GreenNewDeal_Final_v2_12MB.pdf

Sunrise received a collaborative grant from USCAN[356] with Power Shift Network, SustainUS and the Deep South Center for Environmental Justice. Another primary funder thus far of Sunrise is the Sustainable Markets Foundation. The Sunrise address is shared with US Climate Action Network and Sierra Club (50 F St NW, Washington, DC 20016), where Sunrise trainings have been held by USCAN board members.

> *"One factor working in their favor was that the group didn't start from scratch. Some of the architects of the Sunrise Movement included activists from organizations such as 350.org — which also provided some early financial support." — Inside the Sunrise Movement (it didn't happen by accident), December 3, 2018*[357]

Prior to the Sunrise Movement, the framework of a youth-led mobilization in service to capital expansion had already been identified by those at the helm. In that role, people such as Jamie Margolin, youthful founder of Zero Hour, were developed by the establishment. In being trained by the likes of Al Gore (founder of Generation Investment with Goldman Sach's David Blood), Margolin was propelled to celebrity status in a mere few months by utilizing magazines that feed the insatiable American appetite for celebrity fetish (Vogue, People, Rolling Stone). This exposure, coupled with social media recognition by "eco celebrities" (individuals with grotesquely indulgent lifestyles yet lionized as environmental stewards due to their comparatively menial philanthropic endeavours, such as Leonardo DiCaprio) is a tried and true method of manufactured celebrity.

November 6, 2018: Vanity Fair, Alexandria Ocasio-Cortez

356 https://issuu.com/uscan/docs/uscan_annual_report_2017_issuu
357 https://www.eenews.net/stories/1060108439

Across the Atlantic Ocean, more celebrities and groups that would lead "the public into emergency mode" would soon follow.

In June 2018, a Twitter account and an Instagram account were created under the name Greta Thunberg.

In July 2018, a Twitter account was created under the name Extinction Rebellion.[358]

## THE GREEN NEW DEAL IS IN VOGUE

Marketing to a key "femographic", the Green New Deal is today in vogue.

Vogue, November 2, 2018:[359] "Bria Vinaite Explains the Green New Deal: 'Let Vinaite fill you in on the rest of the details—and make sure to find out if your candidates support a Green New Deal when you head to the polls. If they don't, maybe you can ask why.'" ["The foundation of Vogue's leadership and authority is the brand's unique role as a cultural barometer for a global audience."]

As this series will demonstrate, young females are the key "femographic" for the AOC campaign.

It is here where the machinations for the Green New Deal – the vehicle for unlocking 100 trillion dollars, and the long-awaited financialization of nature, begins to unfold.

On November 2, 2018 the Vogue Runway Twitter account shared a promotional video for the Green New Deal featuring celebrity Bria Vinaite. ["Bria Vinaite explains the Green New Deal in the latest #NowYouKnow.] "Liking" the Vinaite tweet was Greg Carlock, architect of the Green New Deal[360], Green New Deal research director and senior advisor to Data for Progress[361] [362], and manager for climate action and Data for World Resources Institute (WRI)[363] where he leads the development of the WRI Climate Program's flagship platform—Climate Watch[364] [365]. Prior to joining WRI, Carlock worked at USAID on greenhouse gas accounting and data.

358 [Further reading: The Increasing Vogue for Capitalist-Friendly Climate Discourse: http://www.theartofannihilation.com/mckibbens-divestment-tour-brought-to-you-by-wall-street-part-xiii-the-increasing-vogue-for-capitalist-friendly-climate-discourse/]

359 https://www.vogue.com/article/now-you-know-bria-vinaite-explains-green-new-deal-midterms

360 https://www.gregcarlock.com/press/

361 https://www.dataforprogress.org/who-we-are/

362 "Greg is Green New Deal Research Director at Data for Progress. He holds a Masters in Environmental Policy and is a researcher in climate action and data based in Washington D.C. He specializes in greenhouse gas accounting, U.S. climate and energy policy, and online data platform development. Greg uses his brain for analysis and leaves the data science to the experts.' [Source: https://www.dataforprogress.org/who-we-are/]

363 https://www.wri.org/profile/greg-carlock

364 https://www.climatewatchdata.org/pathways/models

365 https://www.linkedin.com/in/greg-carlock-666766141/

Also crafting the Green New Deal is Emily Mangan, policy advisor for Data for Progress and research analyst[366] at World Resources Institute. Mangan provides research support and analysis for the Green New Deal. Prior to joining WRI, Mangan worked at the Council on Foreign Relations.[367]

Here it must be made clear that the Ocasio-Cortez and Green New Deal frenzy is part and parcel of the strategy of "leading the public into emergency mode" launched in 2018. In reality, the Green New Deal is window dressing for what is in store. All decisions regarding all "new deals" will not be made by Ocasio-Cortez, the Democrats or any other party. Rather they will be made (and already have been made) by those that comprise the absolute ruling class.

## WORLD RESOURCES INSTITUTE

December 11, 2009: World Resources Institute

April 7, 2011: World Resources Institute

September 12, 2014: World Resources Institute

366 https://www.wri.org/profile/emily-mangan
367 https://www.linkedin.com/in/emily-mangan-1610aa94/

The World Resources Institute (WRI) is a global research non-profit organization that was founded in 1982 by James Speth[368] with a 15 million USD grant from the MacArthur Foundation. It is an international powerhouse "that works in more than 50 countries, with offices in Brazil, China, Europe, India, Indonesia, Mexico and the United States. WRI's more than 500 experts work with leaders to address six urgent global challenges at the intersection of economic development and the natural environment: food, forests, water, climate, energy and cities."

The WRI advisory board represents the absolute upper echelons of power within the matrix of the non-profit interlocking directorate – with a staggering amount of overlap with the hegemonic powerhouse, the Council on Foreign Relations.

With 98.5 million USD in funding in 2017, the exhaustive list of WRI donors[369] represent many of the most powerful and influential entities on Earth, including: Alcoa Foundation, Bloomberg Philanthropies, Cargill, Caterpillar Foundation, Citi Foundation, ClimateWorks Foundation, Bill & Melinda Gates Foundation, William and Flora Hewlett Foundation, John D. and Catherine T. MacArthur Foundation, Gordon and Betty Moore Foundation, Oak Foundation, Rockefeller Brothers Fund, Rockefeller Foundation, Shell Foundation, USAID, and the World Bank.[370]

---

368 https://www.wri.org/profile/james-gustave-speth
"Professor Speth currently serves as honorary director at the Natural Resources Defense Council and World Resources Institute and is on the boards of the Climate Reality Project, the Center for a New American Dream, and the New Economy Coalition. He is an advisory board member at United Republic, 350.org, EcoAmerica, Labor Network for Sustainability, New Economy Working Group, SC Coastal Conservation League, Environmental Law Institute, Vermont Natural Resources Council, Southern Environmental Law Center, Heinz Center, Free Speech for People, Vermont Institute for Natural Science, the Northwest Earth Institute, and the Carbon Underground." [Source: https://www.wri.org/profile/james-gustave-speth]
Speth also serves on the advisory board of The Climate Mobilization [Featured in ACT IV of this series]

369 "Acknowledging Our Donors | Major Donors: Grants and gifts of $750,000 or more, includes revenue received 10/1/16 – 1/15/18 and older grants still open as of 10/1/16" : Alcoa Foundation • Bloomberg Philanthropies • C40 Cities Climate Leadership Group • Cargill, Incorporated • Caterpillar Foundation • The Children's Investment Fund Foundation • Citi Foundation • ClimateWorks Foundation • Department for Business, Energy & Industrial Strategy of the United Kingdom • Department of Foreign Affairs and Trade of Australia • DOB Ecology • DOEN Foundation • Energy Agency of Sweden • European Climate Foundation • European Commission • Federal Ministry for Economic Cooperation and Development of Germany (BMZ) • Federal Ministry for the Environment, Nature Conservation and Nuclear Safety of Germany (BMU) • FedEx Corporation Ford Foundation • Bill and Melinda Gates Foundation • German Agency for International Cooperation (GIZ) • Good Energies Foundation • Google Inc. • William and Flora Hewlett Foundation • IKEA Foundation • Inter-American Development Bank (IDB) • Irish Aid – Department of Foreign Affairs and Trade • Johnson Controls International plc • Linden Trust for Conservation • The John D. and Catherine T. MacArthur Foundation
Ministry for Europe and Foreign Affairs of France • Ministry of Economic Affairs and Climate Policy of the Netherlands • Ministry of Foreign Affairs of Denmark (Danida) • Ministry of Foreign Affairs of the Netherlands (DGIS) • Ministry of Infrastructure and Water Management of the Netherlands • Gordon and Betty Moore Foundation • Charles Stewart Mott Foundation • The Nature Conservancy • Norway's International Climate and Forest Initiative (NICFI) • Norwegian Agency for Development Cooperation (Norad) • Norwegian Ministry of Climate and Environment • Norwegian Ministry of Foreign Affairs • Oak Foundation • Open Society Foundations • Michael Polsky Family • Rockefeller Brothers Fund • Rockefeller Foundation • Stephen M. Ross Philanthropies • Shell Foundation • Skoll Global Threats Fund • Swedish International Development Cooperation Agency (Sida) • Swiss Agency for Development and Cooperation (SDC) • Ruth McCormick Tankersley Charitable Trust • The Tilia Fund • U.K. Department for International Development (DFID) • U.K. Foreign and Commonwealth Office (UKFCO) • United Nations Environment Programme (UNEP) • U.S. Agency for International Development (USAID) • Villum Foundation • The World Bank • Anonymous

370 [WRI 2017 Annual Report: https://wriorg.s3.amazonaws.com/s3fs-public/uploads/wri-2017-annual-report.pdf]

The WRI board of directors[371] include:

• David Blood[372]: Co-founder and senior partner of Generation Investment

• Felipe Calderón[373]: Former president of Mexico, chair of the Global Commission that oversees the New Climate Economy,[374] honorary chairman of the Green Growth Action Alliance

• Christiana Figueres[375]: Executive secretary of the UNFCCC, The B Team leader,[376] vice-chair of the Global Covenant of Mayors for Climate and Energy, board member of ClimateWorks, World Bank Climate Leader, Mission2020 Convenor, member of the Rockefeller Foundation Economic Council on Planetary Health, credited with delivering the Paris Agreement [Full bio][377]

• Jennifer Scully-Lerner[378]: Vice president, private wealth management at Goldman Sachs

• James Gustave Speth[379]: Founder of WRI, former administrator of the United Nations Development Programme, honorary director at the Natural Resources Defense Council and WRI, serves on the board of The Climate Reality Project, advisory board member at 350.org, member of the Council on Foreign Relations

• Andrew Steer[380]: President and CEO of the WRI. Formerly with the World Bank, serves on the sustainable advisory groups of both IKEA and the Bank of America and the Executive Board of the UN Secretary General's Sustainable Energy For All Initiative

• Kathleen McLaughlin[381]: Senior vice president and chief sustainability officer at Walmart Inc., president of Walmart Foundation

• Nader Mousavizadeh[382]: Co-Founder and partner of Macro Advisory Partner, former chief executive of Oxford Analytica, a leading global analysis and advisory firm, former investment banker at Goldman Sachs, member of the Council

371 Susan Tierney: former Assistant Secretary for Policy at the U.S. Department of Energy;
Pamela P. Flaherty: Former president and CEO, Citi Foundation, former director of corporate citizenship, Citi;
Harriet C. Babbitt: Former U.S. Ambassador to the Organization;
Tammie Arnold: formerly with Generation Investment Management;
Frances Beinecke: Former President, Natural Resources Defense Council (NRDC), United States;
Other members include Stephen Brenninkmeijer, Robin Chase, William Chen, Tiffany Clay, Dino Patti Djalal, Alice F. Emerson, Jonathan Lash, Joaquim Levy, Kathleen McLaughlin, Nader Mousavizadeh, Michael Polsky, Bill Richardson, Stephen M. Ross, William D. Ruckelshaus and Roger W. Sant.
[Full board of directors: https://www.wri.org/about/board]

372 https://www.wri.org/profile/david-blood

373 https://www.wri.org/profile/felipe-calderón

374 http://newclimateeconomy.net/about/members-global-commission

375 https://www.wri.org/profile/christiana-figueres

376 http://www.bteam.org/press/global-climate-change-leader-christiana-figueres-joins-the-b-team/

377 https://christianafigueres.com/#/

378 https://www.wri.org/profile/jennifer-scully-lerner

379 https://www.wri.org/profile/james-gustave-speth

380 https://www.wri.org/profile/andrew-steer

381 https://www.wri.org/profile/kathleen-mclaughlin

382 https://www.wri.org/profile/nader-mousavizadeh

of the European Council on Foreign Relations, member of the World Economic Forum's Global Future Council on Geopolitics, WEF Global Leader for Tomorrow

• James Harmon[383]: Chairman and CEO of Caravel Management, member of the Council on Foreign Relations

• Afsaneh M. Beschloss[384]: Founder and CEO of RockCreek. Former managing director and partner at the Carlyle Group and president of Carlyle Asset Management, treasurer and chief investment officer at the World Bank, formerly with Shell International and J.P. Morgan, member of the World Economic Forum's Investor Governors, member of the Council of Foreign Relations, recognized as one of American Banker's Most Powerful Women in Banking

• Joke Brandt[385]: Secretary General of The Ministry of Foreign Affairs of The Netherlands

• Jamshyd N. Godrej[386]: Chairman of Aspen Institute – India. He is the Vice President of World Wide Fund for Nature – International and was the President of World Wide Fund for Nature – India from 2000 to 2007

• Caio Koch-Weser[387]: Chairman of the Board of the European Climate Foundation. Former vice chairman of Deutsche Bank Group, held high-level positions in the World Bank, member of the Global Commission on the Economy and Climate (NCE) and a Member of the Board of the Centre for European Reform (CER) in London[388]

WRI donors include the Federal Ministry for the Environment, Nature Conservation and Nuclear Safety of Germany, William and Flora Hewlett Foundation, IKEA Foundation – in partnership with Agence Française de Développement, the Grantham Foundation for the Protection of the Environment and BlackRock – which led the Climate Finance Partnership[389] (announced September 26, 2018 at the One Planet Summit in NYC by French President Emmanuel Macron and BlackRock's Larry Fink). The accompanying Blended Finance Taskforce,[390] an embodiment of the world's most powerful and financial institutions, is well represented at WRI.

383 https://www.wri.org/profile/james-harmon
384 https://www.wri.org/profile/afsaneh-m-beschloss
385 https://www.wri.org/profile/joke-brandt
386 https://www.wri.org/profile/jamshyd-godrej
387 https://www.wri.org/profile/caio-koch-weser
388 [WRI Global Leadership Council: https://www.wri.org/about/global-leadership-council]
389 https://europeanclimate.org/governments-and-philanthropies-announce-ground-breaking-partnership-with-blackrock-to-mobilize-and-deploy-climate-finance-at-scale/
390 https://www.blendedfinance.earth/steering-committee/

April 27, 2017: World Resources Institute

The Blended Finance Taskforce was launched by Paul Polman's Business & Sustainable Development Commission[391] in 2017. The Commission, created to implement the UN Sustainable Development Goals ("Global Goals"), was funded by institutions, foundations, and corporations including the UN, World Bank, the Bill and Melinda Gates Foundation, and Unilever. The Commission, created to implement the UN Sustainable Development Goals ("Global Goals"), was funded by institutions, foundations, and corporations including the UN, World Bank, the Bill and Melinda Gates Foundation, and Unilever.

The efforts put forward by the Business & Sustainable Development Commission[392] led to the Blended Finance Taskforce, announced on September 26, 2018, paving the way for the Climate Finance Partnership.

Polman is the CEO of Unilever, and chair of both the International Chamber of Commerce and The B Team (co-founder of We Mean Business). Polman has also been closely involved in the implementation of the Sustainable Development Goals (SDGs).[393] The Blended Finance Taskforce was established in order to identify barriers to the effective use and scaling of blended finance.[394] It is now implementing an ambitious plan of action to increase mainstream private investment for the SDGs.[395]

391 http://businesscommission.org/
392 http://businesscommission.org/our-work/blended-finance-taskforce-for-the-global-goals
393 "Since 2009, Chief Executive Officer, Unilever; leading the company to set out an ambitious vision to decouple its growth from overall environmental footprint and increase its positive social impact. Actively seeks cooperation with other companies to implement sustainable business strategies and drive systemic change. Has been closely involved in global discussions on the Sustainable Development Goals (SDGs) and action to tackle climate change. Former Member: High Level Panel on the Post-2015 Development Agenda, presenting recommendations on behalf of the private sector; International Council, Global Commission on the Economy and Climate, under former Mexican President, Felipe Calderon. 2016, asked by the UN Secretary-General to be Member, SDG Advocacy Group, tasked with promoting action on the 2030 Agenda. Chairman, World Business Council for Sustainable Development. Member: International Business Council, World Economic Forum; B Team; Board, UN Global Compact; Business and Sustainable Development Commission. Recipient of numerous awards, including: Climate Visionary Award (2017); Ordre national de la Légion d'honneur (2016); UN Foundation's Champion for Global Change Award (2014); Oslo Business for Peace Award (2015); UN Environment Programme's Champion of the Earth Award (2015)." [Source: https://www.weforum.org/agenda/authors/paul-polman/]
394 http://www.socialwatch.org/node/18095
395 [Full list of Business & Sustainable Development Commissioners including Avaaz co-founder Ricken Patel: http://businesscommission.org/commissioners]

Unilever is a member of WRI's Corporate Consultative Group.[396] WRI member companies include: Abbott Laboratories, Bank of America, Cargill Corporation, Caterpillar, CitiGroup, Colgate-Palmolive, DuPont, General Motors, The Goldman Sachs Group, Google, Kimberly-Clark, PepsiCo, Pfizer, Shell, Walmart, Walt Disney Company, and Weyerhaeuser.[397]

On November 15, 2018,[398] the Climate Markets and Investment Association reported that the parties that comprise the Climate Finance Partnership would "work together to finalize the design and structure of what we anticipate will be a flagship blended capital investment vehicle by the end of the first quarter, 2019." All media inquiries pertaining to this announcement were to be directed to Climate Nexus[399] (People's Climate March) or the European Climate Foundation. The task of the Blended Finance Taskforce is to unlock 100 trillion dollars to rescue the current economic system that has now entered the late stage of "freefall". [Disclosed in ACT IV of this series.] The required maximization and mobilization of public monies for private profits, to save the capitalist economy and further privatization,[400] will be achieved through the climate emergency strategy that has been put into action.

Here it is critical to recognize that the New Climate Economy is a project of the WRI.[401]

396 https://www.wri.org/our-work/project/wri-corporate-consultative-group
397 https://www.wri.org/business/join-corporate-consultative-group-ccg
398 https://www.cmia.net/news/the-climate-finance-partnership-mobilizing-institutional-capital-to-address-the-climate-opportunity/
399 https://www.macfound.org/grantees/2322/
400 http://www.theartofannihilation.com/purpose-goes-to-latin-america-part-i/
401 https://www.wri.org/our-work/project/new-climate-economy

## THE NEW CLIMATE ECONOMY

Kitty v/d Heijden
@KittyvdHeijden
Follow

NCE team president Calderon, Chad Holliday & Andrew Steer @WorldResources meeting NL ministers Ploumen and Mansveld

6 Retweets 2 Likes

January 20, 2015: World Resources Institute, New Climate Economy Team

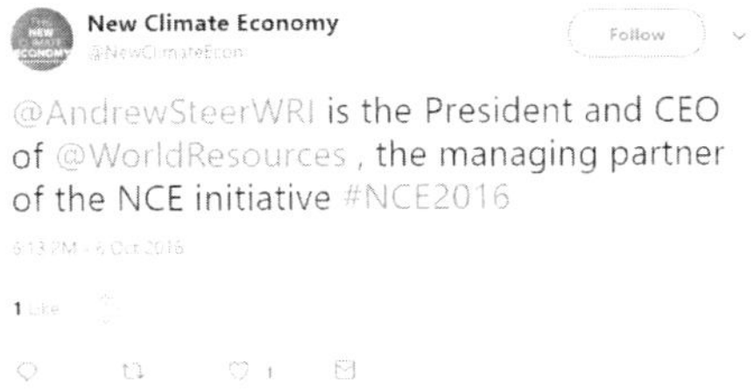
New Climate Economy
@NewClimateEcon
Follow

@AndrewSteerWRI is the President and CEO of @WorldResources , the managing partner of the NCE initiative #NCE2016

1 Like

October 6, 2016: New Climate Economy, World Resources Institute

The New Climate Economy project is led by Helen Mountford, program director for the New Climate Economy project and director of economics at WRI. Other team members from WRI include Milan Brahmbhatt, senior fellow at WRI, and Molly McGregor, research coordinator in the President's office at WRI.[402]

The New Climate Economy project is being "conducted by a team of economists and policy and business analysts drawn from, and supported by, a partnership of nine leading global economic and policy institutions" under the direction of WRI.

Research partners for the initiative are as follows: Climate Policy Initiative,[403] Ethiopian Development Research Institute,[404] Global Green Growth Institute,[405] Indian Council for Research on International Economic Relations,[406] London School of Economics and Political Science,[407] Overseas Development Institute,[408] Stockholm Environment Institute,[409] and Tsinghua University.[410]

The New Climate Economy initiative works with global institutions including the International Monetary Fund, International Energy Agency, Organisation for Economic Co-operation and Development and UN agencies. It is overseen by a global commission comprising former heads of government, finance ministers, a plethora of the *crème de la crème* of economics, business and finance.[411]

The New Climate Economy Global Commission members include Felipe Calderón[412] (honorary chair), Paul Polman[413] (co-chair), Angel Gurría,[414] Nicholas Stern[415] (co-chair), Sharan Burrow[416] and many other members overlapping with the WRI, Climate Finance Partnership, Blended Finance Taskforce, etc. A cabal so entrenched in corporate power that it can easily make one's head not only spin, but explode.[417] The demand for citizen groups is

402 [New Climate Economy Global Project Team: http://newclimateeconomy.net/content/project-team]
403 https://climatepolicyinitiative.org/
404 http://www.edri.org.et/
405 http://gggi.org/
406 http://icrier.org/
407 http://www.lse.ac.uk/home.aspx
408 https://www.odi.org/
409 https://www.sei-international.org/
410 http://www.tsinghua.edu.cn/publish/newthu/index.html
411 [Economic Advisory Panel: http://newclimateeconomy.net/content/economics-advisory-panel]
[Emeritus Commissioners: http://newclimateeconomy.net/about/emeritus-commission-members]
412 http://newclimateeconomy.net/about/global-commission/felipe-calderón-hinojosa
413 https://newclimateeconomy.net/about/global-commission/paul-polman
414 http://newclimateeconomy.net/about/global-commission/angel-gurría
415 http://newclimateeconomy.net/about/global-commission/nicholas-stern
416 http://newclimateeconomy.net/about/global-commission/sharan-burrow
417 Ngozi Okonjo-Iweala, Chad O. Holliday, Suma Chakrabarti, Helen Clark, John Flint, Kristalina Georgieva, Jamshyd Godrej, Stephen Green, Sri Mulyani Indrawati, Dr. Agnes Kalibata, Naina Lal Kidwai, Caio Koch-Weser,

ironic seeing as the financialization of nature is happening behind closed doors – with a promissory note of silence from the non-profit industrial complex.

The Green New Deal is tied to WRI. WRI is the New Climate Economy. The last and the most important piece of the puzzle is the Natural Capital Coalition.

Here it is imperative to note that the Natural Capital Coalition[418] is comprised by those at the helm of the New Climate Economy and WRI.

## "NEW DEAL FOR NATURE" – ASSIGNING MONETARY VALUE TO ALL OF NATURE

*"The financial value at stake is mind-boggling – and the business opportunities likely to be created by the shift in the prevailing market paradigm are astonishing.... Who will be the Bill Gates of ecosystem services?" — The Biosphere Economy, 2010*

In tandem with orchestrating a frenzy over a Green New Deal via the non-profit industrial complex and media mechanisms, WWF[419] et al were quietly pushing forward with a "New Deal for Nature". The Green New Deal conjures up images of wind turbines and solar panels that are miraculously perceived as natural and holistic. [The fact that a solar panel and wind turbine has become more strongly associated with nature and environment than an actual tree, insect or animal is, in itself, quite terrifying and a stark indicator in the power of social engineering conducted on the citizenry over the last two decades.] This feat, achieved via powerful branding and NGO association,[420] serves as the bright green mask for the even more sinister deal – the financialization of Nature – reframed as the "New Deal for Nature".

---

Ricardo Lagos, Frannie Leautier, Patricia de Lille, Carlos Lopes, Takehiko Nakao, Christian Rynning-Tønnesen, Kristin Skogen Lund, Jean-Pascal Tricoire, Maria van der Hoeven and Chen Yuan http://newclimateeconomy.net/about/members-global-commission/

418 https://naturalcapitalcoalition.org/in-2020-we-need-a-new-deal-for-nature/

419 https://www.dailymotion.com/video/x105tsl

420 http://www.eartheconomics.org/

January 26, 2018: "New Deal For Nature", WWF

Yet, it's not new at all, with the Natural Capital Project (NatCap) having been launched in 2006 and its affiliate, the Natural Capital Coalition, which was formerly the TEEB for Business Coalition[421] (prior to 2014). NatCap and its two NGO partners – WWF and The Nature Conservancy – were involved in the Natural Capital Coalition from the onset.

NatCap was founded by Stanford University [Stanford Woods Institute for the Environment[422] and the Department of Biology[423]], The Nature Conservancy, World Wildlife Fund, and the Institute on the Environment of the University of Minnesota. The scope of its global network[424] includes corporations such as Coca-Cola and Dow Chemical, and institutions such as the US Department of Defense and the World Bank.

The scope of the Natural Capital Coalition[425] is a massive conglomerate of corporate power, including many NGOs and so-called conservation bodies.[426]

Here we can add that "Harnessing the Fourth Industrial Revolution for the Earth", published by the World Economic Forum's "System Initiative on Shaping the Future of Environment and Natural Resource Security" is a partnership with PricewaterhouseCoopers and the Stanford Woods Institute for the Environment.[427]

421 https://wiki.p2pfoundation.net/TEEB_for_Business_Coalition
422 https://woods.stanford.edu/research/centers-programs/natural-capital-project
423 https://ccb.stanford.edu/
424 https://naturalcapitalproject.stanford.edu/collaborators/
425 https://naturalcapitalcoalition.org/who/coalition-organizations/?mfilter=all
426 https://naturalcapitalcoalition.org/who/coalition-organizations/?mfilter=conservationbodies
427 http://www3.weforum.org/docs/WEF_Harnessing_the_4IR_for_the_Earth.pdf

*"Taken all together, the value of the total global ecosystem services has been estimated at USD 125 trillion per year, which is almost twice the world's gross domestic product."—Natural Capital Coalition, July 12, 2018*[428]

The development of the Natural Capital Protocol Project was made possible with generous funding from the Gordon and Betty Moore Foundation, International Finance Corporation (World Bank) with the support of the Swiss State Secretariat for Economic Affairs (SECO) and the Ministry of Foreign Affairs of the Government of Netherlands, The Rockefeller Foundation, United Nations Environment Programme (UNEP), and the UK Department for the Environment, Food and Rural Affairs (DEFRA). The Coalition is hosted by The Institute of Chartered Accountants in England and Wales (ICAEW). Other funders include: World Wildlife Fund, The Nature Conservancy, the Google Foundation, the Inter-American Development Bank, Unilever, The David and Lucile Packard Foundation, U.S. Department of Defense and the World Bank.[429]

World Resources Institute provided the technical insights and review for the Natural Capital Protocol. The protocol was developed by Conservation Interna-

428 https://naturalcapitalcoalition.org/the-value-of-ecosystem-services-from-giant-panda-reserves/
429 https://naturalcapitalproject.stanford.edu/what-is-natural-capital/

tional, The B Team, PricewaterhouseCoopers, Sustain Value, ACTS,[430] Arcadis,[431] eftec,[432] Environmental Resources Management (ERM), Imperial College, ISS, Natural Capital Project, Synergiz, WWF, Accenture, CDSB, Deloitte, Dow, eni, GIST Advisory, Kering, LafargeHolcim, Natura, Nestlé, Roche, Shell, and The Nature Conservancy. The protocol was led by the World Business Council for Sustainable Development (WBCSD) consortium.[433]

Today, the final frontier for the corporate capture of the Earth as a whole, has finally arrived. Other terms thrown into the ring for public acceptance are a "New Deal for Nature and Humanity" and a "New Deal for Nature and People".

> *"The New Deal for Nature[434] is expected to be adopted during the fifteenth meeting in Beijing in 2020." — Biodiversity International, November 30, 2018*[435]

430 https://acts-net.org/rnre-projects/138-natural-capital-protocol
431 https://www.arcadis.com/en/global/
432 https://eftec.co.uk/home
433 https://naturalcapitalcoalition.org/development/
434 https://www.cbd.int/post2020/
435 https://www.bioversityinternational.org/news/detail/how-will-we-finance-the-new-deal-for-nature/

On January 23, 2019[436] the Natural Capital Coalition released an announcement stating that "In 2020, We Need A New Deal for Nature." This article was part of the 2019 World Economic Forum "Shaping the Future of Environment and Natural Resource Security" system initiatives[437]. The authors of the article were Marco Lambertini[438], Director-General, WWF International, Paul Polman[439], CEO of Unilever, and Børge Brende[440], former Foreign Minister of Norway (2013-2017) and president and member of the managing board of the WEF[441].

The urgency in accelerating the plan forward is made clear:

> *"Against this backdrop, we need 2019 to be the year that sees a step-change in mobilising a wider public-private biodiversity action agenda.* ***We need a "New Deal for Nature" to emerge."***

To make this happen, a movement is identified as the vehicle:

> *"A movement has the combined power and influence to be able to identify* ***a simple set of targets for action on nature that everyone can aim for*** *– so-called "science-based targets" to which every business, investor, NGO, city and government can contribute by 2030, such that meeting them will slow down the damage we are doing to nature, and ultimately restore it to the level science says we need."*

Over and over we are inundated with the "simple set of targets" that "everyone can aim for". Hence, we witness the creation of mobilizations, global in scale, with no rational demands whatsoever.

The implementation of the New Deal for Nature will lay the groundwork for payments for ecosystem services (PES). This will create the most spectacular opportunity for monetary gain that the financial sector has ever witnessed. New markets offer speculation that promises unimaginable profits. The commodification of most everything sacred, the privatization and objectification of all biodiversity and living things that are immeasurable, above and beyond monetary measure, will be unparalleled, irreversible and inescapable.

---

436 https://naturalcapitalcoalition.org/in-2020-we-need-a-new-deal-for-nature/
437 https://www.weforum.org/system-initiatives
438 https://www.weforum.org/agenda/authors/marco-lambertini
439 https://www.weforum.org/agenda/authors/paul-polman
440 https://steigan.no/2017/09/borge-brende-far-sin-lonn-i-davos/
441 [WEF Board of Trustees, 2017:
https://www.weforum.org/press/2017/09/norway-s-borge-brende-joins-world-economic-forum/]
[WEF Leadership and Governance:
https://www.weforum.org/about/leadership-and-governance]

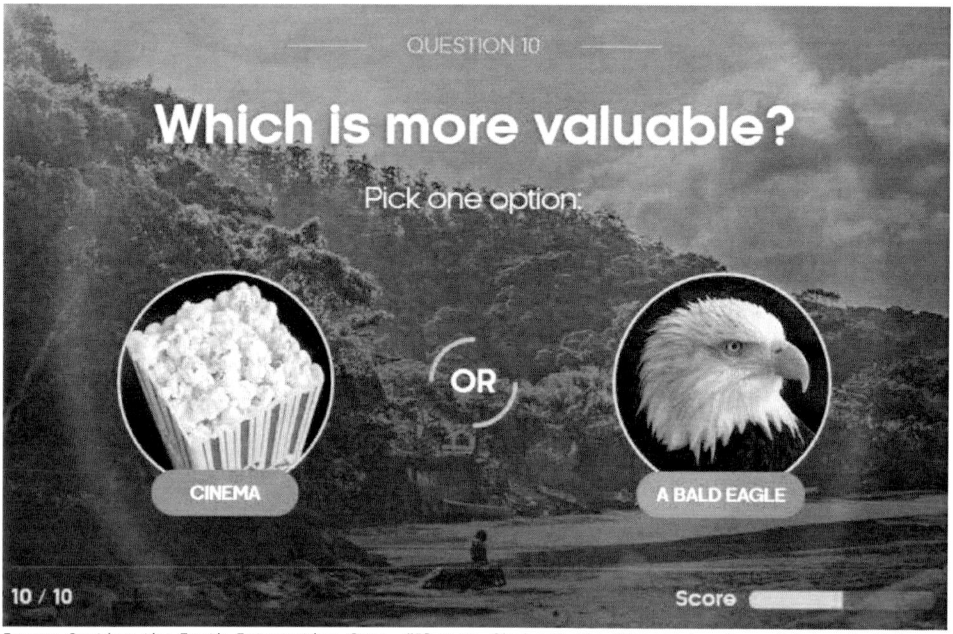

Image: Costing the Earth Interactive Game, "Play to find out the financial value of Nature", BBC, October 8, 2015

In order to manufacture consent from the populace, those rolling out a "new deal for nature" are utilizing the power of holistic language. They are strategically exploiting the very real contempt that we, the public have for *externalities* (e.g. pollution) – only to sell the financialization of nature back to us as a society. This is very much the same method we witness today as the power elites masterfully exploit the discontent of the youth and the population at large.

The New Deal for Nature is the gentle easement[442] of the mental acceptability of the financialization of nature into the public psyche, which is quite rapidly becoming a global phenomenon. So hideous is the payments for ecosystem services (PES) scheme, masked under the holistic phrase "natural capital", that it is barely mentioned outside of closed doors. But if we look closely, we can find it hidden in plain sight.

442 https://wevaluenature.eu/#page5

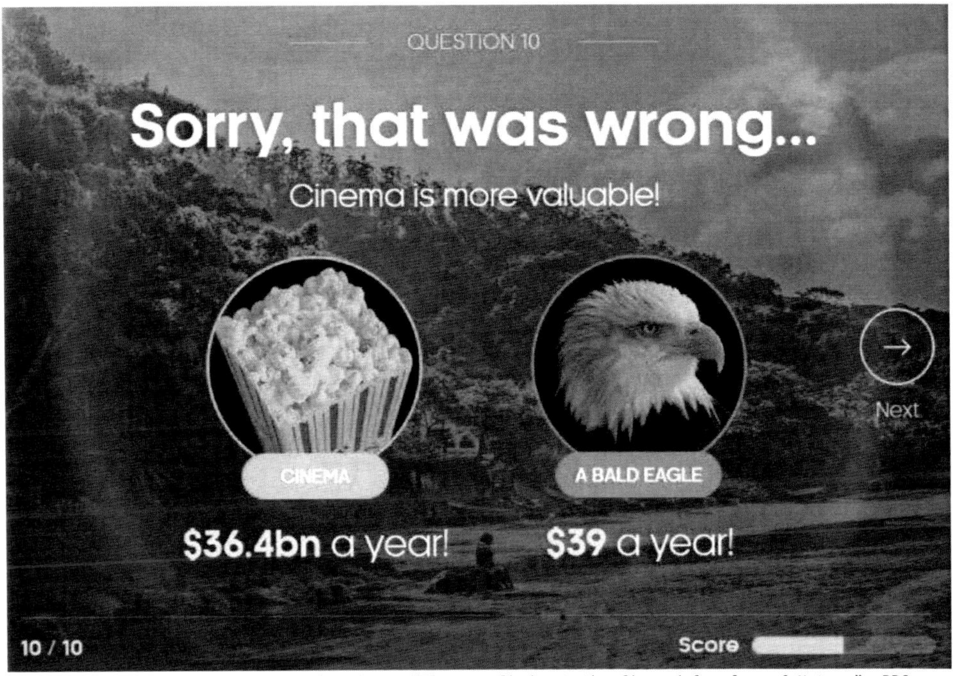

Image: Costing the Earth Interactive Game, "Play to find out the financial value of Nature", BBC, October 8, 2015

May 21, 2018: Science Can Help Forge a New Deal for Nature[443]:

> *"The global community has a unique window of opportunity to define the post 2020 global biodiversity framework.* ***It will need bold commitment and determination, innovative approaches and transformative processes to ensure that such a New Deal will be effective.*** *At this historical juncture, let us leverage science to help* ***forge a New Deal for Nature****." — Christiana Pașca Palmer[444], executive secretary of the Secretariat of the Convention on Biological Diversity*

November 22, 2018: **A New Deal** for Nature and Humanity[445]:

> *"WWF strongly supports the call for a* ***new deal for nature and people****. By 2020,* ***in just two years, we need an agreed roadmap*** *that recognizes the intrinsic link between the health of nature, the well-being of people and the future of our planet."*

443 https://www.thegef.org/blog/science-can-help-forge-new-deal-nature
444 https://www.thegef.org/people/christiana-pașca-palmer
445 http://wwf.panda.org/wwf_news/?339010/Un-nouveau-pacte-pour-la-Nature-et-lhumanite

November 29, 2018: UN Biodiversity Conference Agrees on a **Process Towards a New Deal for Nature and People** in 2020 But Ambition is Weak[446]:

> *"The 14th Conference of the Parties (COP14) of the United Nations Convention on Biological Diversity (CBD) ended today with an agreement on the preparatory process for a post-2020 global framework,* ***moving us closer to a transformational New Deal for Nature and People in 2020*** *– a vital step to ramp up global efforts to halt today's unprecedented and dangerous biodiversity loss.*
>
> ***WWF urges member countries to develop a far higher shared vision and political ambition if we are to reach a New Deal for Nature and People and create a Paris-style moment for biodiversity in 2020."***

Welcome to the Green New Deal, New Deal For Nature, Next System, Regenerative System, New Economy, New Climate Economy, Biosphere Economy, etc. A fusion of rhapsodic and mellifluous language that creates a sublime chrysalis to further expand capital markets. The second verse is the same as the first.

A genuine rebellion against ecological devastation does not – and cannot – turn its back on capitalism,[447] imperialism,[448] militarism, sexism (patriarchy, misogyny) and racism (white supremacy). The main drivers of our accelerating environmental crises. Marching for capital under the guise of marching for revolution is a fool's game. All roads lead to the corporate capture, theft and pillage of what remains of our already decimated planet.[449]

446 http://wwf.panda.org/?339391/UN-Biodiversity-Conference-agrees-on-a-process-towards-a-New-Deal-for-Nature-and-People-in-2020-but-ambition-is-weak
447 https://deepgreenresistance.org/en/
448 http://www.theburningspear.com/
449 [Further reading: Building Acquiescence for the Commodification of the Commons Under the Banner of a "New Economy": http://www.theartofannihilation.com/mckibbens-divestment-tour-brought-to-you-by-wall-street-part-xii-building-acquiescence-for-the-commodification-of-the-commons-under-the-banner-of-a-new-economy/]

# ACT VI

## A DECADE OF SOCIAL MANIPULATION FOR THE CORPORATE CAPTURE OF NATURE [CRESCENDO]

The final act of this series is dedicated to Greta Thunberg and the youth she has inspired across our fragile planet. The upper echelons of power have every intention to capture and channel this energy – and use it to maintain the current power structures. They are already in the process of doing so.

We have reached the Brave New Moment where there is no longer a distinction between our "movements" and the corporate forces that have been created to further our oppression and servitude – all in compliance to economic growth and capitalism for the world's ruling class. All of this to be achieved on the backs of the most vulnerable – our youth. Hegemonic forces are salivating over the global waves of youth mobilization demanding action on climate change.

The paradox is this – the youth are their vehicle. Their resistance sequestered and redirected directly back into the very system that will destroy the same future they march to save. When children from even the wealthiest of families (monetary wealth being the epitome of "success" in the West) are part and parcel of an epidemic of depression in our society – we need to question why we would do *anything* that would prop-up a failing system that benefits so few – at the expense of so much.

Let this knowledge serve as a weapon for resistance.

March 10, 2014:[450]

> *"... the divestment campaign will result (succeed) in a colossal injection of money shifting over to the very portfolios heavily invested in, thus dependent upon, the intense commodification and privatization of Earth's last remaining forests, (via REDD, environmental "markets" and the like). This tour de force will be executed with cunning precision under the guise of environmental stewardship and "internalizing negative externalities through appropriate pricing." Thus, ironically (if in appearances only), the greatest surge in the ultimate corporate capture of Earth's final remaining resources is being led, and will be accomplished, by the very environmentalists and environmental groups that claim to oppose such corporate domination and capture." — McKibben's Divestment Tour – Brought to You by Wall Street [Part II of an Investigative Report, The "Climate Wealth" Opportunists]*

450 http://www.theartofannihilation.com/350-orgs-friends-on-wall-street-the-climate-wealth-opportunists-part-ii-of-an-investigative-report/

## THE CHAPERONE

chap·er·one Dictionary result for chaperone: 1. a person who accompanies and looks after another person or group of people. Synonyms: companion, duenna, protectress, escort, governess, nursemaid, carer, keeper, protector, bodyguard, minder.

For the final segment of this series, let's circle back to where we began. With Greta Thunberg.

During the January 2019 World Economic Forum (WEF) in Davos, Thunberg's celebrity was fully utilized to give those in the public realm an illusion of a newfound "compassionate capitalism". This was especially true for the WEF Ocean Day Programme in which Thunberg was featured on the panel "What Will a Changing Ocean Mean to Us, Our Jobs and Markets?". While those on the panel[451] (including Angel Gurría,[452] Secretary-General, Organisation for

451 https://youtu.be/8Gh_I3SwEwI
452 http://www.wrongkindofgreen.org/2016/01/25/the-de-klein-of-a-revolutionary-writer-from-subcomandante-marcos-to-angel-gurria/

Economic Co-operation and Development) spoke of the ocean as a market at risk ("if we don't save the oceans that is a 24 trillion dollar loss"), Thunberg's innocence created a veneer of legitimacy over the grotesque objectification of nature. Meanwhile, Al Gore sat on the "Taking Action for The Ocean"[453] panel ("the 'ocean economy' is estimated to account for 3% – 5% of global GDP, with assets worth $24 trillion. How can the world tap into the ocean economy while protecting it from environmental collapse?") discussing[454] the global climate strikes (as a pivotal sign of change – approx. 30m:10s in) and the necessity to assign monetary value to nature. Of course, the key pivotal moment for the exploitation of Thunberg (and the very purpose of her global construct) came at the moment she spoke her much-publicized words "Our house is on fire. I'm here to say, our house is on fire." These words echoed the outlined text in the strategy paper entitled, "Leading the Public Into Emergency Mode" almost verbatim. The strategy, authored by the Climate Mobilization Project, outlines a "wartime-style mobilization, akin to the American home front effort during World War II". [ACT IV]

Above: World Economic Forum panel: "What will a changing Ocean mean to us, our jobs and markets?" From left to right: Haley Edwards, moderator, correspondent, TIME Magazine, Sharan Burrow, General Secretary, International Trade Union Confederation, Katherine Garrett-Cox, Gulf International Bank, and Greta Thunberg

453 https://www.weforum.org/events/world-economic-forum-annual-meeting/sessions/taking-action-for-the-ocean
454 https://webcasts.weforum.org/widget/1/davos2019?p=1&pi=1&th=1&hl=english&id=a0W0X00000DXggDUAT

Above: January 25, 2019, Twitter [455]

The above photograph of Thunberg on her way home from Davos was shared on social media on January 25, 2019. The woman accompanying Thunberg in the photo, as well as the person who shared the photograph, is not Thunberg's mother nor her grandmother. Rather, she is Jennifer Morgan, executive director of Greenpeace International. And this is where all the pieces of our elaborate puzzle finally fit into place.

During the gathering, while Thunberg's presence was being exploited in multiple ways, one being an attempt to add both legitimacy and diplomacy to the Oceans conference, Morgan was present at far more intimate discussions – those that focused on the "New Deal for Nature".

455 https://twitter.com/climatemorgan/status/1088881907788582917

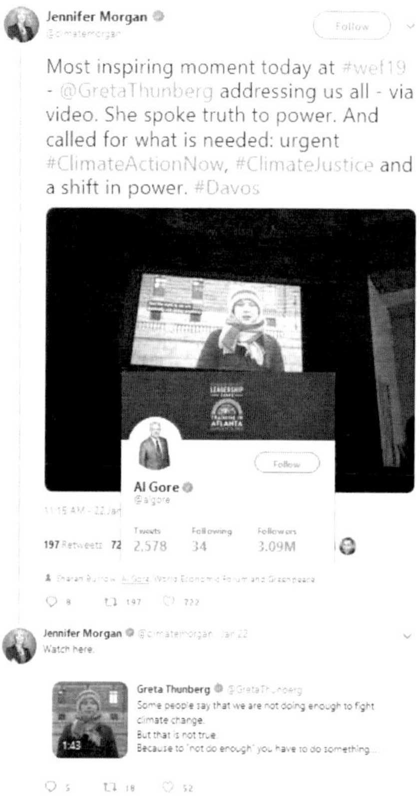


Above: January 22, 2019, Twitter, tagged users: Al Gore, World Economic Forum, Sharan Burrow, Greenpeace International

457

Above: January 24, 2019, Twitter, New Deal For Nature, Global Shapers, World Economic Forum, Davos

456

Above: World Economic Forum YouTube Channel: "Davos 2019 – A New Deal For Nature", published February 9, 2019

458

456 https://twitter.com/Cathy_IV/status/1088603013898559488/photo/1
457 https://twitter.com/climatemorgan/status/1087790934199361536
458 https://www.youtube.com/watch?v=05bG9ovIzDQ

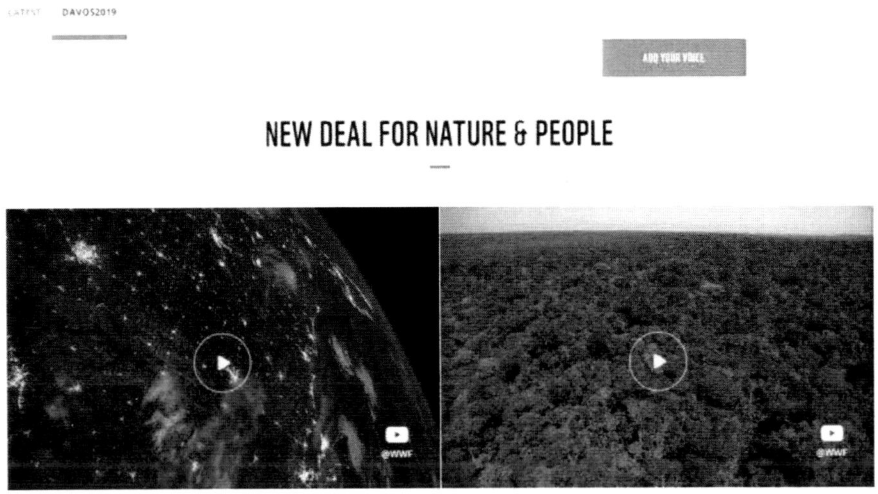


Above: "22-25 January 2019. We're rallying world leaders to act for the planet, our one home. Add your voice to demand for a sustainable future for all. – WWF AT WORLD ECONOMIC FORUM – ADD YOUR VOICE"
459

One not familiar with the inner workings and functions of the non-profit industrial complex might wonder why the executive director of Greenpeace International would be invited to attend a discussion regarding the implementation of "payments for ecosystem services" (PES), global in scale. That is, monetary value being assigned to all nature, under the guise of environmental protection. That is, the financialization and privatization of all nature – on the entire Earth.

And here we must pay attention.

Morgan is the former global climate change director of Third Generation Environmentalism (E3G). Prior to E3G, she led the Global Climate Change Program for the Worldwide Fund for Nature (WWF). Morgan has worked for the US Climate Action Network (USCAN), the European Business Council for a Sustainable Energy Future, and for the Federal Ministry of Environment. She served as senior advisor to the German Chancellor's chief advisor, advised former Prime Minister Tony Blair, and currently serves on Germany's Council for Sustainable Development.

459 https://wwf.panda.org/wwf_news/davos2019/

Above: 1998: "Jennifer Morgan, climate policy officer, WWF, seated with Andrew Kerr, WWF, who presented the WWF report on Climate Change and Human Health" UNFCCC COP-4, THE FOURTH MEETING OF THE CONFERENCE OF THE PARTIES TO THE UN FRAMEWORK CONVENTION ON CLIMATE CHANGE, BUENOS AIRES, ARGENTINA, 2-13 November, 1998
460

But more importantly than all the above job titles is Morgan's role in relationship to the upper echelons of power: her prior position as the global director of the climate and energy program at the World Resources Institute.[461]

The 2019 World Economic Forum (which features Morgan's publications[462] and blog posts on its website) was not the first instance of Morgan's involvement

460 http://enb.iisd.org/climate/ba/nov5se.html
461 [Bio: https://www.weforum.org/people/jennifer-morgan]
[Source: https://www.greenbiz.com/users/jennifer-morgan]
462 https://www.wri.org/profile/jennifer-morgan

in the coming "New Deal For Nature". During the closing remarks of the Global Landscapes Forum[463] on December 9, 2018,[464] at COP24, Morgan stressed that in addition to shifting global focus from the oil and transportation sectors to land and forests, additional co-operation was required to reach consensus on the New Deal for Nature:

> *"We also need much improved cooperation for a new deal for nature to be agreed on at the next CBD cop in 2020 setting decisive biodiversity guidelines for climate action." — Jennifer Morgan, executive director of Greenpeace International – Closing remarks, Global Landscapes Forum, COP24, Dec 9, 2018*[465]

The truth is that Morgan's career as a darling and confidante of the elite establishment has been long established. Her perseverance and sound navigation within the interlocking directorate of the non-profit industrial complex has brought her to this very moment.

Above: May 14, 2013, Jennifer Morgan, Rainer Baake, Lutz Weischer, Carol Browner, World Resources Institute, Flickr

463 https://www.globallandscapesforum.org/about/partners/
464 https://www.globallandscapesforum.org/video/jennifer-morgan-closing-remarks-glf-at-cop24/
465 https://www.globallandscapesforum.org/video/jennifer-morgan-closing-remarks-glf-at-cop24/

466

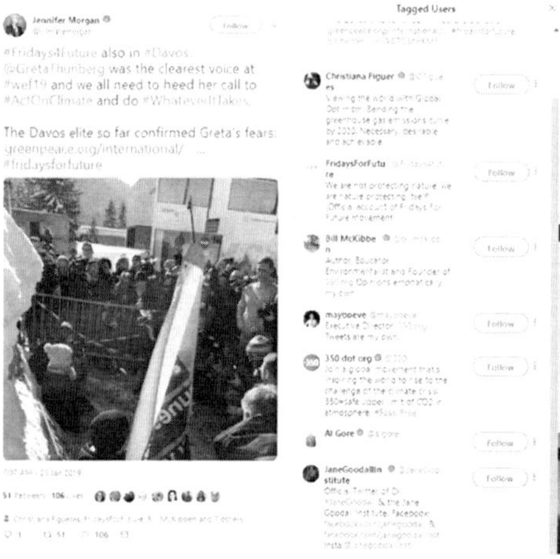


Above: January 25, 2019, World Economic Forum, Davos, Greta Thunberg

Above: Al Gore, New Deal for Nature via the UN Sustainable Development Goals, WEF, Davos, 2019

Above: Former Vice President of the USA, Al Gore (The Climate Reality Project and Generation Investment) and executive director of Greenpeace International, Jennifer Morgan. ClimateHub, COP24, Katowice, Poland.

466 https://www.flickr.com/photos/worldresourcesinstitute/8744971284

467

Above: November 28, 2018: Greenpeace Australia Pacific, Facebook

468

Above: November 3, 2015, Jennifer Morgan (@ClimateMorgan), World Resources Institute, The Climate Group, The Climate Reality Project

ld64
970/10157295353162971

Above: January 23, 2019, Green New Deal

Here it is critical to recognize that the World Resources Institute is a founding partner of Global Campaign for Climate Action (GCCA), and that the New Climate Economy[469] – a project of Global Commission on the Economy and Climate[470] launched in 2013 – is also founded by the World Resources Institute.

What the New Climate Economy is expressing when it states that, "**the shift to a low-carbon and climate-resilient economy is only one – potentially small – part of a much broader economic transition that is under way**" is this: the transformation of global finance via the economic valuation and payment for environmental services.

> *"The failure to price our natural capital, on which our wealth and well-being depends, is a serious failure in the global capital market. Worth many trillions of dollars in financial assets, the global capital market shapes the world we live in, and which our children will inherit." — Kitty van der Heijden, director, World Resources Institute Europe and Africa, Finance for One Planet, 2016*[471]

469 https://www.wri.org/our-work/project/new-climate-economy
470 https://newclimateeconomy.net/about/members-global-commission/
471 http://www.oecd.org/water/OECD-GIZ-Conference-Background-Document-Finance-for-One-Planet.pdf

# BIRDS OF A FEATHER: WORLD RESOURCES INSTITUTE, WORLD WILDLIFE FUND & STOCKHOLM ENVIRONMENT INSTITUTE

> *"Unfortunately, many environmental non-governmental organisations have bought into this illogical reasoning and justify their support as being pragmatic. Neoliberal language is rife across their reports and policy recommendations and their adoption of natural capital, ecosystems services, offsetting and market trading. These new environmental pragmatists believe, without justification, that the financialisation of Nature will help prevent its destruction." — from the paper This Changes Nothing: The Paris Agreement to Ignore Reality*[472] *authored by Clive L. Spash, WU Vienna University of Economics and Business, Vienna, Austria*

472 https://www.clivespash.org/wp-content/uploads/2015/04/2016-Spash-This-Changes-Nothing.pdf

Above: November 14, 2017, "Stronger Together for Climate Action". L-R: Paul Polman, CEO, Unilever, Pascal Canfin, CEO, WWF France, Jennifer Morgan, Executive Director, Greenpeace International; Ramiro Fernández, Director of Climate Change at Fundacion Avina; Manuel Pulgar-Vidal, Global Leader, WWF Climate and Energy Practice; and Edmund Gerald Brown, Jr., Governor of California. Photo: IISD/ENB, Herman Njoroge Chege
[473]

> *"We need the CBD [Climate Change and Biodiversity] to attain* ***the highest political relevance*** *and develop a far higher shared vision* ***if we are to reach a New Deal for Nature and create a Paris-style moment*** *for biodiversity in 2020." — November 15, 2018,*[474] *media release, WWF Rallies Behind the Call for a New Deal for Nature and People [Emphasis added]*

As discussed in ACT V of this series, the board of directors overseeing the World Resources Institute represent the very upper tiers of the ruling class.

Also disclosed was that Helen Mountford is the program director for the New Climate Economy project and director of economics at World Resources Institute. Prior to this appointment, Mountford served as deputy director of environment for the Organisation for Economic Co-operation and Development (OECD). Beyond its formal research partnerships,[475] the New Climate Economy

473 http://enb.iisd.org/climate/cop23/stronger-together/
474 https://www.worldwildlife.org/press-releases/wwf-rallies-behind-the-call-for-a-new-deal-for-nature-and-people
475 https://newclimateeconomy.net/content/research-partners

is aligned with the World Bank, International Monetary Fund, International Energy Agency, regional development banks, UN agencies and the OECD.

World Resources Institute is a key co-founder in the social engineering apparatus,[476] GCCA (TckTckTck), which officially launched in 2008. Long before the elite forces declarations of a climate emergency that we witness unfolding today, scientists and academia had already recognized that the industrial scale of our collective objectification and destruction of nature had proceeded to such scale, it threatened the collapse of industrial civilization (exploiting and enslaving most – for the benefit of few). Of course, long before this, the Indigenous could see the writing on the wall as the European pursued his conquering of nature in blind earnest.

Markets have finally conquered the Western world. Our society is now maxed out on debt and economic growth has not only stagnated, it is on a downward spiral. Today, we find ourselves in a culture so disconnected from reality that it considers economic growth far more valuable than the planetary ecosystems that sustain all life.

As this series has demonstrated and will further demonstrate in this closing segment, the GCCA coalition was designed, financed and orchestrated by the same entities now set to unlock 100 trillion USD and simultaneously implement the privatization and financialization of nature via the New Deal For Nature (payments for ecosystem services) to be agreed upon by 2020. As demonstrated in ACT IV – the urgency we bear witness to today, is due to a fear far greater than the collapse of the planetary biosphere, that is – the collapse of the capitalist economic system.

World Resources Institute, World Wildlife Fund, and the New Climate Economy are at the helm of the financialization of nature. Also at the helm is the Natural Capital Coalition (collaborating with both World Resources Institute and World Wildlife Fund), which represents over 300 of the world's most powerful and egregious corporations while engaging "many thousands more".[477]

The New Climate Economy research partner, the Stockholm Environment Institute has a well-oiled revolving door between itself and the World Wildlife Fund. The institute has generous funding to the tune of 260 million SEK in 2017[478] (approx. 28 million USD) including almost ten million SEK from the Bill & Melinda Gates Foundation. As a side note, we can add that the Stockholm Environment Institute gave a presentation at a climate function on May 4, 2018 ("Welcome to the Power of Capital")[479] with both Ingmar Rentzhog, CEO

476 https://si2gallery.wordpress.com/
477 https://naturalcapitalcoalition.org/who/coalition-organizations/
478 https://www.sei.org/wp-content/uploads/2018/04/j5928-sei-annual-report-180424-web-2-smallest.pdf
479 http://www.vipevent.nu/spp/

of We Don't Have Time and Malena Ernman (WWF Environmental Hero Award, 2017, and Thunberg's mother.)

On November 21, 2017[480] it was announced that Pavan Sukhdev was appointed as president of WWF International: "Pavan Sukhdev, former director of the UN Environment Initiative for a Green Economy, has been appointed President of WWF International." Sukhdev, former managing director of the Markets Division of Deutsche Bank, would launch the findings of the TEEB[481] study in 2010, the acronym standing for 'The Economics of Ecosystems and Biodiversity,' an initiative of the United Nations Environment Programme (UNEP). The Natural Capital Coalition[482] was formerly the TEEB for Business Coalition.

> *"Stockholm is home to two institutions, the Stockholm Resilience Centre and Stockholm Environment Institute, which have done a great deal of research to better understand and apply the concepts of Natural Capital to the way we manage ecosystems and the economy. Johan Rockström, executive director of the Stockholm Resilience Centre, and a group of 28 academics proposed a new Earth system framework in 2011 for government and management agencies to use as a tool to support sustainable development." — Stockholm: Natural Capital of the World, September 23, 2019*[483]

On February 13, 2019,[484] The Guardian published the article, *School Climate Strike Children's Brave Stand Has Our Support.* "We are inspired that our children, spurred on by the noble actions of Greta Thunberg and other striking students, are making their voices heard, say 224 academics". Those endorsing the letter included Annemarieke de Bruin, researcher, Stockholm Environment Institute, Dr Alison Dyke, Stockholm Environment Institute, Dr Jean McKendree, Stockholm Environment Institute and Corrado Topi, ecological economist, Stockholm Environment Institute.

480 https://www.wwf.fr/vous-informer/actualites/pavan-sukhdev-est-nomme-president-du-wwf-international
481 https://youtu.be/iN_BuEjUppw
482 http://www.naturalcapitalcoalition.org/
483 https://www.naturalcapitalpartners.com/news-media/post/stockholm-natural-capital-of-the-world
484 https://www.theguardian.com/environment/2019/feb/13/school-climate-strike-childrens-brave-stand-has-our-support

## A DECADE OF STRATEGIC AND METHODICAL SOCIAL ENGINEERING

> *"Citizen protests and legal actions against companies, governments and individuals will undoubtedly become an increasing leverage opportunity in support of this emergency approach and have already begun." — Club Of Rome 'The Climate Emergency Plan', launched with We Don't Have Time and Global Utmaning, December, 2018*

Above: TckTckTck Flickr: "The Press Conference of the 'Beds are Burning' Launch in Paris was well attended as Kofi Annan, David Jones, Mélanie Laurent, Manu Katché and many other supporters of the campaign made their appearance."

> *"The objective was to make it become a movement that consumers, advertisers and the media would use and exploit." — TckTckTck Havas Pager*[485]

GCCA (TckTckTck) was founded by a small group of NGOs, including: World Resources Institute (WRI), 350.org, Greenpeace, Avaaz and World Wildlife Fund. It is partnered with over 470 members, including ClimateWorks[486] (founded in 2004 by the Hewlett, Packard and McKnight foundations), which is discussed further on in this segment. Climate Week NYC 2014 (September 22–26), an annual initiative of the Climate Group,[487] was marketed in conjunction

485 http://canadianclimateaction.files.wordpress.com/2010/01/tck-havas-pager.pdf
486 https://www.climateworks.org/about-us/people/our-board/
487 https://www.theclimategroup.org/

with the People's Climate March that took place on September 21, 2014. Climate Week NYC[488] was founded in 2009 as a partnership between The Climate Group, the United Nations, the UN Foundation, GCCA/TckTckTck, the Carbon Disclosure Project,[489] the Government of Denmark and the City of New York.

The march was organized by GCCA/TckTckTck, the Rockefeller Brothers Fund, Climate Nexus (a sponsored project of Rockefeller Philanthropy Advisors), 350.org (incubated by the Rockefeller Foundation), the Rasmussen Foundation and USCAN.

The Climate Group business campaigns "are brought to you as part of the We Mean Business coalition."[490]

> *"The Strategic Plan 2018–2022 lays out WRI's approach and priorities for the next five years.* ***WRI's approach is to help catalyze and advance non-incremental shifts in policy and behavior, unusual political, social and corporate partnerships, to be understood in the context of "movements" rather than policy shifts.*** *" — Ministry of Foreign Affairs, Concept Note, Support to World Resources Institute, Implementation of the Strategic Plan 2018–2022*[491]

Through the GCCA/TckTckTck coalition, a decade of social engineering went unnoticed. The September 21, 2014 People's Climate March and the global marches that would follow, such as Rise Up mobilizations, "Work Parties", Power Shift gatherings, etc. etc. had multiple purposes with multiple desired effects which were incredibly successful for those at the helm. To "Change Everything We Need Everyone"[492] was a signal. A behavioural engineering cue that would coalesce a camaraderie between the citizenry and corporate power to become "stronger as one". All focus would be kept far away from the key drivers of climate change (militarism, the capitalist economic system dependent on infinite growth and exploitation, industrial agriculture/*livestock, etc.) which could be made to be, like the Indigenous–led 2010 People's Agreement of Cochabamba,[493] invisible. Instead, this energy would be directed to the discourse of "clean energies" as the singular most important solution for our mul-

488 https://www.climateweeknyc.org/
489 http://www.theartofannihilation.com/mckibbens-divestment-tour-brought-to-you-by-wall-street-part-xiii-the-increasing-vogue-for-capitalist-friendly-climate-discourse/
490 https://www.wemeanbusinesscoalition.org/
[Source: https://www.climateweeknyc.org/climate-week-nyc-opening-ceremony-initial-speakers-announced]
491 https://www.google.de/url?sa=t&rct=j&q=&esrc=s&source=web&cd=2&ved=2ahUKEwi7-OTR-ZfhAhWLYVAKHaNyCjUQFjABegQIABAC&url=http%3A%2F%2Fum.dk%2Fen%2F~%2Fmedia%2FUM%2FEnglish-site%2FDocuments%2FDanida%2FAbout-Danida%2FDanida%2520transparency%2FConsultations%2F2017%2FWRI.pdf&usg=AOvVaw0gRbftNDs1i_a0N-y6NMZf
492 http://www.wrongkindofgreen.org/2015/10/02/financing-the-message-behind-naomi-kleins-this-changes-everything-project/
493 https://pwccc.wordpress.com/2010/04/24/peoples-agreement/

tiple ecological crises. The belief in two objects was sufficient for an entire populace to be reassured that there would be zero sacrifice. The Western lifestyle could continue unabated. The solar panel and wind turbine directive took centre stage. The crowd roared in applause. The singular focus of "renewable energy" became an eco-fetish of the Western populace, the targeted demographic. [*sentient beings, formerly recognized as animals.]

The ten-year social engineering effort also led to a transition from environmentalism into full-blown yet undetected anthropocentrism.[494] Over a ten–year span, "environmentalism"[495] moved from that of protecting nature, to demanding a roll-out of green technology, industrial in scale, that would further plunder nature. The natural world became irrelevant as the desire for green technology superseded environmental protection. Wind turbines and solar panels replaced images of trees and insects as the new symbols of our natural world. Saving the industrial civilization that is killing off all life, became paramount to saving the ecosystems that all life depends on. These ideologies slowly took hold until "movements" become nothing more than lobby groups for green energy. Volunteers marching for capital, global in scale. To suggest that Edward Bernays would be impressed would be an understatement. Such is the beauty of social engineering and behavioural change.

Yet to fully understand how we arrived at today's dismal precipice, we must first revisit the past.

In 2009, over a span of five months, GCCA/TckTckTck and affiliated partners registered 15.5 million names worldwide on its online petition for a "fair, ambitious and binding climate change agreement." Many marketing firms outside of Havas helped achieve this, including the corporate communications and public affairs agency Hoggan & Associates[496] of which DeSmogBlog co-founder Jim Hoggan is president and founder. Hoggan's client list[497] includes corporate creation TckTckTck,[498] Canadian Pacific Railway, Shell and ALCOA. DeSmogBlog may "expose" Shell on occasion, yet Hoggan & Associates has no problem raking in Shell cash to, in their own words, "...help clients identify the optimum frame and establish it in the public mind.[499]

494 http://www.theartofannihilation.com/standing-rock-profusion-collusion-big-money-profits-part-6-conclusion/
495 http://www.wrongkindofgreen.org/2018/01/06/environmentalism-and-democracy-in-the-age-of-nationalism-corporate-capitalism/
496 http://www.hoggan.com/
497 https://www.hoggan.com/our-clients
498 https://web.archive.org/web/20150213105703/https:/www.hoggan.com/tcktcktck
499 http://www.theartofannihilation.com/keystone-xl-the-art-of-ngo-discourse-part-ii/

*"THE MOST PRESSING ENVIRONMENTAL PROBLEM WE FACE TODAY IS NOT CLIMATE CHANGE. It is pollution in the public square, where a smog of adversarial rhetoric, propaganda and polarization stifles discussion and debate, creating resistance to change and thwarting our ability to solve our collective problems." — Jim Hoggan, co-founder of DeSmogBlog [Source: Hoggan & Associates]*[500]

[Further reading: EYES WIDE SHUT | TckTckTck exposé, January 6, 2010[501]]

The day before the international climate negotiations kick off in Cancun, the global TckTckTck campaign and its partners presented UNFCCC executive secretary Christiana Figueres Photo: Ivan Castaneira/tcktcktck

Kelly Rigg, executive director of Tck Tck Tck, speaks during the opening ceremony of Climate Week NYC in New York, September 20, 2010. (Photo by Ramin Talaie/Corbis via Getty Images)

500 https://www.hoggan.com/publications
501 https://www.counterpunch.org/2019/02/25/slandering-the-not-so-radical-green-new-deal-a-bipartisan-operation/

In 2014, Kelly Rigg, executive director of TckTckTck from 2009–2014, was credited as the key organizer for the 2014 People's Climate March:

> *"Large groups, like 350.org, Avaaz or the Sierra Club, and the numerous grassroots organizations (1,300 by some estimates) don't just start magically working together to rent buses, secure police permits and make signs specific to their interests. There has to be a vision into which they all buy, a big enough umbrella under which everyone can stand. Building that umbrella—particularly for the international organizations—was Rigg's work, work that includes important leadership lessons relevant to anyone trying to mobilize large groups with diverse interests and agendas.* ***Her work can be seen as a road map for how to herd cats."*** *Forbes, Sept 25, 2014:*[502] *Leadership Lessons from The People's Climate March [Emphasis added.]*

Prior to her role at GCCA/TckTckTck, Rigg served as deputy campaigns director for Greenpeace International from 1998-2003, and as its project coordinator from 1982–1993.[503] In addition, Rigg is founding director of the international consultancy, Varda Group[504] co-founded in 2003 with Rémi Parmentier. GCCA/TckTckTck is identified as a Varda client, as is Greenpeace, Ceres (divestment partner),[505] Amnesty International, and Friends of the Earth, WWF, Nature Conservancy, WCBSD, UNEP, etc.[506]

Having started his career at Friends of the Earth France, Parmentier also holds an extensive history[507] with Greenpeace spanning 27 years, as well as extensive relations with multilateral bodies:

> *"Rémi Parmentier has been involved in the process of Rio +20 from the start. He participated in the intersession meetings and the Preparatory Committee in New York with "informal consultations" on behalf of various international organizations and alliances. Previously, as the Political Director of Greenpeace International, in the Summit of Johannesburg* ***in 2002, Parmentier was the negotiator and protagonist of the agreement between the World Business Council for Sustainable Develop-***

502 http://www.forbes.com/sites/toddessig/2014/09/25/leadership-lessons-from-the-peoples-climate-march/
503 https://www.linkedin.com/in/kellyrigg/?originalSubdomain=ca
504 http://www.vardagroup.org/about-us-kelly-rigg
505 http://www.theartofannihilation.com/mckibbens-divestment-tour-brought-to-you-by-wall-street/
506 [Client List: http://www.vardagroup.org/our-clients]
507 http://regardssurlaterre.com/en/author/remi-parmentier

***ment and Greenpeace International on the Kyoto Protocol.***'[508] *[Emphasis added]*

Parmentier also served as deputy executive secretary for the Global Ocean Commission[509] (2013–2016) which was launched[510] in February 2013. Inés de Águeda, who serves as the communications officer for the Global Ocean Commission, is also an associate at the Varda Group.

Commissioners[511] of the Global Ocean Commission have included José María Figueres (co-chair), President of Costa Rica from 1994 to 1998, brother of Christina Figueres, former president of the Carbon War Room, David Miliband[512]; John Podesta[513], chair of the Center for American Progress and a former White House chief of staff; Sri Mulyani Indrawati, managing director at the World Bank; Pascal Lamy, director-general of the World Trade Organization and other high profile individuals.[514]

Here we can add that José María Figueres served as a director of the World Wildlife Fund, the World Resources Institute, and the Stockholm Environment Institute. He was also the first CEO of the World Economic Forum and later served as CEO of Concordia 21.[515]

[Further reading: Under One Bad Sky | TckTckTck's 2014 People's Climate March: This Changed Nothing, September 23, 2015][516]

And the following information would too come as no surprise, if only the populace could see through the fog of faux environmentalism.

Alnoor Ladha is a founding partner and the head of strategy at Purpose.[517] With its expertise in behavioural change, Purpose is most renowned for its White Helmets cam-

508 https://www.revistaesposible.org/phocadownload/esposible26_eng.pdf
509 http://www.globaloceancommission.org/about-the-commission/partners/
510 https://twitter.com/kellyrigg/status/298341963109920769
511 http://www.globaloceancommission.org/the-commissioners/
512 http://www.theguardian.com/politics/2006/dec/11/uk.greenpolitics
513 http://www.globaloceancommission.org/news/press-releases/john-podesta-joins-global-ocean-commission/
514 http://www.globaloceancommission.org/news/press-releases/launch-of-commission/
515 http://www.theartofannihilation.com/purpose-goes-to-latin-america-part-i/
[Source: https://www.rmi.org/people/jose-maria-figueres/]
516 http://www.theartofannihilation.com/under-one-bad-sky-tcktcktcks-2014-peoples-climate-march-this-changed-nothing/
517 https://redefineschool.com/alnoor-ladha/

paign[518] – a 21st century hybrid-NGO[519] serving NATO states. Ladha is a founding member and the executive director of the Purpose project, The Rules. Ladha serves on the board of Greenpeace USA, where its executive director, Annie Leonard, has co-founded Earth Economics.[520] Yet another institution created to aid, abet and, most importantly, profit off the financialization of nature scheme, now well underway as demonstrated in this series. Leonard's Earth Economics[521] [4] is a member of divestment partner CERES, which is in turn a partner of the World Business Council for Sustainable Development (WBCSD). Purpose (PR arm of Avaaz) manages The B Team (co-founder of We Mean Business) the official address of which, is the office of Purpose.

The link between most, if not all of these NGOs, institutions and high-level individuals, is the shared desire for carbon markets and/or the implementation of payments for ecosystem services (PES).

Above: Kelly Rigg, founding director, Varda Group, US: The Economics of Sustainable Development, 16-19 June, 2012 | Rio de Janeiro, Brazil, Photo: International Institute for Sustainable Development (IISD) website

518 https://www.unmultimedia.org/avlibrary/asset/2338/2338981/
519 http://www.theartofannihilation.com/the-humanitarian-industrial-complex-school-of-thought-a-fish-analogy/
520 http://www.eartheconomics.org/
521 "Earth Economics, with the support of our Community Partners and Advisors, maintains the largest, spatially explicit, web-based repository of published and unpublished economic values for ecosystem services. With generous funding from our sponsors, in 2012 Earth Economics began porting our internal database to a web-based service. The Ecosystem Service Valuation Toolkit (EVT) portal was launched at Rio +20 in June 2012. The Researcher's Library and SERVES were previewed at the ACES Conference in December 2012."

*"Since the 1970s, several waves of privatization have swept the world. In 2017, the Privatization Barometer concluded that "the massive global privatization wave that began in 2012 continues unabated". According to the rights expert, that wave has been driven not only by Governments and the private sector, but also by international organizations, especially the International Monetary Fund (IMF), the World Bank and the United Nations." — Human rights at risk from tsunami of privatization, Third World Network, November 16, 2018*[522]

*"The second issue is the issue of reductions of emissions. There must be radical reductions of emissions starting from now. In our view, by 2017 we should cut, developed countries must cut by 52%, 65% by 2020, 80% by 2030, well above 100 [percent] by 2050. And this is very important because the more you defer action the more you condemn millions of people to immeasurable suffering." — Lumumba Di-Aping, chief negotiator of the G77, December 11, 2009,*[523] *COP15*

In 2008, as the global climate change director for E3G, Jennifer Morgan (executive director, Greenpeace International) played a central role and lead catalyst in the formation and launch of the GCCA – the aforementioned coalition first conceptualized in 2006.[524] With extensive experience in the United Na-

522 https://www.twn.my/title2/unsd/2018/unsd181102.htm
523 https://www.youtube.com/watch?v=zOEG3M7dlDo
524 "Officially launched in 2008, the GCCA's origins date back to April 2006 when representatives from some of the largest environmental and developmental groups—Oxfam, Greenpeace International, Greenpeace Brazil, WWF

tions Framework Convention on Climate Change (UNFCCC) process, Morgan was the ideal choice.

"With an overall budget of USD 6.8 million—over 95 % of which came from foundation funding—the GCCA was undoubtedly the most well-funded global climate campaign of 2009." Grants for the 2009 GCCA/TckTckTck campaign (created by Havas Worldwide/Euro RSGG[525] in collaboration with Kofi Annan's[526] Global Humanitarian Forum) morphed to eleven million USD.[527]

In 2013, the International Policies and Politics Initiative (IPPI) was established by five foundations: the European Climate Foundation (ECF), ClimateWorks Foundation, Oak Foundation, the Children's Investment Fund Foundation (CIFF) and the Mercator Foundation. The initiative would act "as a platform where foundations and grantees meet to strategize on how international political and policy levers can catalyse more ambitious policies at the domestic level." The ClimateWorks Foundation was largely operated by the McKinsey & Company, an acting advisor to Richard Branson's Carbon War Room.[528]

The GCCA would greatly benefit the IPPI:

> *"The GCCA and the TckTckTck campaign offer a potent example of how foundation funds—and most significantly those of the Oak Foundation—were mobilized for capacity building purposes in the run-up to Copenhagen."*[529]

---

International, WWF India, the World Council of Churches, Friends of the Earth and the Union of Concerned Scientists—convened in Woltersdorf (Germany) to discuss the possibility of developing a common platform to mobilize the wider public and thereby bolster the climate negotiations." [p. 70]
"In 2009, its core funders were the Oak Foundation, the Sea Change Foundation, the Turner-affiliated Better World Fund, the Prince Albert II Foundation of Monaco and the Government of Québec. With a total contribution ofUSD 5 million in 2009, the Oak Foundation was by far the GCCA's main donor (the Sea Change Foundation coming second with USD 1.5 million). [p.69]
It was founded on "[connecting] the intelligence gathering and sophisticated advocacy provided by numerous NGOS in order to target and maximize the collective impact of groups on every continent" (GCCA 2009)." [p.71]
[Source: The Price of Climate Action-Philanthropic Foundations in the International Climate Debate, published in 2016 by Edouard Morena]

525 https://havas.com/

526 https://www.un.org/sg/en/content/kofi-annan

527 The GCCA made over USD 3 million worth of grants to partner organizations in support of their communications and campaigning activities. As they explain in their 2009 Annual Report, 'most grants were awarded to support national and regional campaigning (including for rapid response actions and national hubs), with the remaining funds for global campaign and communication actions'. In other words, the GCCA, while not a foundation per se, acted as a de facto regranting organization, selectively distributing funds to push through a common message. What is more, GCCA grants had a leveraging effect by enabling partners to mobilize further funding—both internally and externally—for GCCA-related activities. According to its 2009 Annual Report, 'partners reported a further total of more than eight million in funds leveraged from their own organisations plus additional sources for activities carried out with financial support from the GCCA'. [Source: The Price of Climate Action-Philanthropic Foundations in the International Climate Debate, published in 2016 by Edouard Morena] [p.72]

528 "IPPI is presented as "a new platform for philanthropic cooporation to catalyse greater ambition on climate through activities and processes taking place at an international level" (ECF 2014, 26). It is "designed to help philanthropy identify opportunities for international collaboration, develop joint strategies, and pool and align grant making to achieve greater overall impact." It acts as a platform where foundations and grantees meet to strategize on how international political and policy levers can catalyse more ambitious policies at the domestic level. [Source: The Price of Climate Action-Philanthropic Foundations in the International Climate Debate, published in 2016 by Edouard Morena] [p. 5]

529 [Source: The Price of Climate Action-Philanthropic Foundations in the International Climate Debate, 2016, https://www.palgrave.com/gp/book/9783319424835], [p. 73]

Morgan, by this time serving with the World Resources Institute, was the ideal person to coordinate the IPPI platform in the run-up to and during the 2015 United Nations Climate Change Conference (COP21) held in Paris. Morgan was chosen to lead IPPI due to her vast experience in the international climate realm coupled with her World Resources Institute (WRI) affiliation. In essence, this was a signal to corporate power that its interests would be protected. ["The WRI, given its director's links with governments and international institutions like the World Bank, was seen as a legitimate partner in the eyes of the funders."][530]

And while IPPI and GCCA controlled the "movement", the same forces also controlled the message via the Carbon Briefing Service (CBS)[531]. The news service was launched by Jennifer Morgan (WRI) and Liz Gallagher (E3G) in late 2014 with additional funding by the ClimateWorks Foundation, the Hewlett Foundation, the Oak Foundation, the Villum Foundation and Avaaz.[532]

The description[533] on the E3G website describes CBS as "a joint E3G-WRI Platform providing political analysis and intelligence to a wide range of actors in the run up to the Paris 2015 climate change negotiations". Consider that the communications distributed via the CBS "ownerless" network began with the following notice: "This briefing is confidential and not for public circulation. You have received it due to your relationships with CBS members and networks." Invitation only CBS participants included: Iain Keith (Avaaz), Jamie Henn (350), Camilla Born (E3G), Liz Gallagher (E3G), Mohamed Adow (ChristianAid), Monica Araya, Martin Kaiser (Greenpeace Germany), Farhana Yamin (TrackO), Wael Hmaidan (CAN International), Bill Hare (Climate Analytics), Pascal Canfin (WRI), Michael Jacobs (Grantham), Alden Meyer (UCS), Tim Nuthall (ECF), Alix Mazounie (RAC-France).[534]

> ***"IPPI is focused on using the 'Paris moment' to increase the scale and pace of change."*** *— Jennifer Morgan, World Resources Institute*[535]

By utilizing GCCA, IPPI, CBS and outside "progressive media", in conjunction with collaborating NGOs and institutions that comprise the non-profit industrial complex, the creation of the "Paris moment" would be achieved.

530 [Source: The Price of Climate Action-Philanthropic Foundations in the International Climate Debate, 2016, https://www.palgrave.com/gp/book/9783319424835], [p. 101]
531 https://www.cbs-climate.org/
532 Ibid.
533 https://www.e3g.org/people/victoria-harris
534 https://www.palgrave.com/gp/book/9783319424835
535 Ibid, p.5

Havas Worldwide (creator[536] of the TckTckTck campaign) was recognized as a convening partner of the COP21 Earth To Paris campaign with collaborating partners identified as 350.org and Avaaz (GCCA/TckTckTck founders), Ceres, The Climate Reality Project, The Nature Conservancy, We Mean Business, the World Bank (via Connect4Climate) and a host of others. Long before the conference had even concluded it was announced that during a live-streamed summit on December 7 and 8, the Earth To Paris partners would deliver "a new universal climate change agreement."

United Nations Development Programme Press Release,[537] October 29, 2015:

> *"Earth To Paris, a coalition of partners helping to drive awareness about the connection between people and planet as well as the need for strong climate action, announced it will host "Earth To Paris—Le Hub" a two-day, high-impact, live-streamed summit on 7 and 8 December in Paris during COP21 — the United Nations climate conference[538] to deliver a new universal climate change agreement."*

The fact that a "new universal climate change agreement" was announced on October 29, 2015, a month prior to the conference actually taking place, was lost on the populace.[539]

> *"As the establishment rave in Paris winds down, the chimera of clean energy[540] propels industrial societies toward nuking the future.[541] The new age ghost dance,[542] as an expression of social despair, has led to progressive self-delusion[543] that promises us the world, if only we believe.[544] Stepping through the looking glass,[545] one can examine the metrics of messaging[546] by establishment social media and philanthropy, that, combined, is the driving force*

536 https://web.archive.org/web/20170708085057/http:/www.newswire.ca/news-releases/kofi-annans-open-source-tcktcktck-campaign-supported-by-over-1-million-people-538236651.html

537 http://www.undp.org/content/undp/en/home/presscenter/pressreleases/2015/10/29/earth-to-paris-le-hub-two-day-summit-will-convene-experts-advocates-influencers-and-ceos-to-discuss-climate-action-during-cop21.html

538 http://www.undp.org/content/undp/en/home/presscenter/events/2015/december/COP21-paris-climate-conference-firstversion.html

539 [From TckTckTck, to Air France, to "Earth To Paris", Havas Worldwide Continues to Hypnotize: http://www.wrongkindofgreen.org/2015/12/01/from-tcktcktck-to-air-france-to-earth-to-paris-havas-worldwide-continues-to-hypnotize/]

540 http://acultureofimbeciles.com/2014/09/never-land-the-chimera-of-clean-energy/

541 https://intercontinentalcry.org/nuking-the-future/

542 https://intercontinentalcry.org/new-age-ghost-dance/

543 http://publicgood.org/2014/09/progressive-self-delusion-from-hope-and-change-to-this-changes-everything/

544 http://publicgood.org/2014/09/if-only-we-believe-the-new-green-economy/

545 http://www.wrongkindofgreen.org/2012/09/11/through-the-looking-glass/

546 http://www.wrongkindofgreen.org/2015/11/30/metrics-as-a-proxy-for-social-change-the-climate-cartel-impact-funding-and-the-abandonment-of-struggle/

*of the non-profit industrial complex. — Jay Taber, Rave New World*[547]

IPPI, as co–ordinated by Morgan, was created as a "discrete ECF programme" which would "work behind the scenes." "While the ECF had given rise to the original idea and while it housed its dedicated staff, IPPI was very much presented as an autonomous and "unbranded" initiative ("unbranded" as in not linked to any particular organization").[548]

*"Although civil society groups are assumed to be normatively motivated [...] they are nonetheless embedded in a global capitalist economy and have quite specific material requirements that must be fulfilled in order to operate successfully." — Lipschutz and McKendry, Social Movements and Global Civil Society, August, 2011*[549]

Lipschutz and McKendry (quoted above) further elaborate: "to be successful, an organization must survive and, in a market–based environment, this means finding ways to generate the funds necessary to sustain operations".[550] Yet, it is more than this. Those at the helm, as this series has demonstrated, share the same ideologies and Western mindsets as the capitalists and corporations whose interests they serve.

The IPPI brought together the influential players: Greenpeace, WWF, 350.org, Avaaz, CAN International, Oxfam, E3G, The Climate Group and the World Resources Institute. The formation of GCCA was one commonality between many of these NGOs and think tanks coupled with extensive involvement in the international climate arena, coupled with strong affiliations with negotiators and the UNFCCC secretariat.[551]

*"The role of Avaaz is particularly revealing in this respect. In other words, it was not a case of promoting one approach among many but of making sure that the IPPI approach was the only approach while maintaining a false sense of pluralism both inside and on the margins of the climate negotiations. Core contributors*

547 http://www.wrongkindofgreen.org/2015/11/30/metrics-as-a-proxy-for-social-change-the-climate-cartel-impact-funding-and-the-abandonment-of-struggle/

548 https://www.palgrave.com/gp/book/9783319424835

549 http://www.oxfordhandbooks.com/view/10.1093/oxfordhb/9780199566600.001.0001/oxfordhb-9780199566600-e-25

550 Funds are required to both finance participation and facilitate lobbying activities— through joint initiatives, platforms, dialogues, reports, campaigns, outreach activities, and the creation and upholding of informal relationships of trust between NGOs and the UNFCCC secretariat and/or members of government delegations (Caniglia et al. 2015 , 241; Caniglia 2001 ; Dodds and Strauss 2004 ). [Source: The Price of Climate Action-Philanthropic Foundations in the International Climate Debate, published in 2016 by Edouard Morena] [p. 6]

551 Ibid. [p. 101 and p. 118]

*to the IPPI strategy went to extraordinary lengths to prevent fellow non-state actors from "getting in the way" of a positive diplomatic outcome in Paris." — The Price of Climate Action-Philanthropic Foundations in the International Climate Debate, 2016, Edouard Morena]*[552]

## THE KEY FOUNDATIONS

To be clear, the IPPI is not the only case of foundation involvement and influence in the climate policy realm. However, it is one of the most "successful", given how influential it has proven to be. Most policies (if not all) are driven by corporations via the largest and most influential foundations and think tanks created and financed by profits from these very same corporate entities.

The field of climate philanthropy regroups a fairly small number of large players. A 2010 study for the Foundation Center showed that in 2008, 25 foundations accounted for over 90% of all climate change funding. More recent data from the same source discloses that six foundations—Oak, Packard, Hewlett, I Sea Change, Energy, Rockefeller—accounted for approximately 70% of climate change policy funding in 2012.[553]

In 1989, Environmental Defence Fund, WWF and Greenpeace, with foundation backing, launched the Climate Action Network (CAN) which Jennifer Morgan also presided over in her career at USCAN. One foundation, the Rockefeller Brothers Fund, which financed regional offshoots of CAN, would comment in its 1993 annual review, that these "global preachers" "played a central role beginning in the early days of the climate change debate".[554]

It is here that we must jump forward to the present day.

In the article "Philanthropy Teams Up With Institutional Investors to Fight Climate Change," published on September 7, 2017,[555] the need for a new approach that will unlock capital for new climate infrastructure at scale is highlighted:

> *"[B]ecause climate change represents such an extraordinary threat, it's imperative we compress the dynamics of innovation and scale through new approaches. That's why Planet Heritage Foundation...*[556] *a global investment advisory firm that works with*

552 https://www.palgrave.com/gp/book/9783319424835
553 Ibid., p. 10
554 Ibid., p. 32
555 https://pndblog.typepad.com/pndblog/2017/09/philanthropy-teams-up-with-institutional-investors-to-fight-climate-change.html
556 http://www.planetheritage.org/

*institutional investors to channel capital into "climate infrastructure" sectors such as clean energy, water, and waste-to-value. These investors — sovereign funds, pensions, endowments, insurance companies, family offices, and foundations — represent more than $80 trillion in assets and are the only stakeholders other than governments with the capacity to invest at a scale... After only a year,* ***the Aligned Intermediary model*** *is already demonstrating promise in this regard...*

*"In partnership with Sarah Kearney (PRIME)[557] and Alicia Seiger (**Stanford University**),[558] we initially attracted grant funding totaling $500,000 from four philanthropies — the **Hewlett Foundation**,[559] the **MacArthur Foundation**,[560] the **ClimateWorks Foundation**,[561] and Planet Heritage Foundation — for research that demonstrated the potential of our model." [Emphasis added]*

One year later, at the One Planet Summit in NY on September 26, 2018[562], the Climate Finance Partnership, a group co–ordinated by the Task Force on Philanthropic Innovation and Aligned Intermediary, announced the new instruments for unlocking capital at scale:

*"Efforts to blend capital in order to engage and mobilize large-scale institutional capital toward climate solutions took a notable step forward on September 26 at the One Planet Summit in New York, when French President Emmanuel Macron and BlackRock's Larry Fink announced the Climate Finance Partnership (CFP).[563] The CFP consists of a unique combination of philanthropies, governments, institutional investors, and a leading global asset manager. The parties, including **BlackRock**, **the Governments of France and Germany**, and the **Hewlett**, **Grantham**, and IKEA foundations, have committed to work together to finalize the design and structure of what we anticipate will be a flagship blended capital investment vehicle by the end of the first quarter, 2019.*

557 http://primecoalition.org/
558 https://energy.stanford.edu/people/alicia-seiger
559 htttp://www.hewlett.org/
560 https://www.macfound.org/
561 http://www.climateworks.org/
562 https://www.atlanticcouncil.org/blogs/energysource/the-climate-finance-partnership-mobilizing-institutional-capital-to-address-the-climate-opportunity
563 https://europeanclimate.org/governments-and-philanthropies-announce-ground-breaking-partnership-with-blackrock-to-mobilize-and-deploy-climate-finance-at-scale/

*The partnership, coordinated by the Task Force on Philanthropic Innovation and the **Aligned Intermediary**,*[564] *an investment advisory group, was designed and structured specifically to use a layer of government and philanthropic capital to maximize private capital mobilization toward climate-related sectors in emerging markets." [Emphasis added]*

The Blended Finance Taskforce (ACT IV of this series) comprises fifty icons of finance including the MacArthur Foundation (World Resources Institute), the Rockefeller Foundation and the ClimateWorks Foundation.[565]

The same article sheds light on the "violent agreement" to unlock $100 trillion USD:

*"A detailed analysis*[566] *by the World Bank found that while **$100 trillion is held by pension funds** and other institutional investors, these same investors allocated less than $2 trillion over a 25 year period into infrastructure investment in emerging markets. And the fraction of that investment that could be considered green, clean, or climate-friendly was negligible.*

*So, what can be done? Whether you choose to look through the lens of unprecedented challenge or unprecedented opportunity, **there is violent agreement that institutional capital needs to be "unlocked"** (a favorite word on the climate conference circuit) and **mobilized quickly and at scale**." [Emphasis added]*

The foundations involved in climate policy from inception, which continue to work hand-in-hand with select NGOs and NGO leaders, are the same foundations to benefit from the Climate Finance Partnership. The roadmap to unlocking 100 trillion dollars is identified in pension funds. The roadmap to the privatization and financialization of nature, global in scale, is the interlocking directorate of the non-profit industrial complex, a matrix of overlapping highways of hegemony.

On December 12, 2017, at the One Planet Summit, Frank Bainimaramai, COP23 President and Prime Minister of Fiji, stated:[567]

*"...after all when we talk about tapping into the vast amounts of institutional capital for climate solutions we are largely talking*

564 http://alignedintermediary.com/
565 [Full list: https://www.blendedfinance.earth/steering-committee/]
566 https://library.pppknowledgelab.org/documents/5450?ref_site=kl
567 https://www.youtube.com/watch?v=EB8HzBcIaRg&t=3s

*about the retirement savings of ordinary hard-working citizens and we need to honor the expectation of being good stewards with the money..."*

To be clear: The money for multi-billion-dollar corporations – to create privatized services and industries, under the guise of environmental protection, is going to be PAID FOR BY THE PUBLIC – BUT THE PUBLIC WILL NOT OWN THEM. For this would be communism – a detestable idea in the Western world. For the corporate sector, it's no risk – all profit. Anything that fails – the public is on the hook.

John D. Rockefeller once stated that, "the ability to deal with people is as purchasable a commodity as sugar or coffee and I will pay more for that ability than for any other under the sun." Truer words were perhaps never spoken.

The skill and precision in achieving the protection and expansion of the capitalist economic system is today nothing less than extraordinary. By utilizing the non-profit industrial complex, the world's most powerful oligarchs need not force their will onto society. Rather, akin to what Aldous Huxley prophesized in his fictional novel Brave New World, we have been manipulated and engineered to demand the very "solutions" that will further empower those that destroy us.

*"The climate Glitterati, such as, M. Bloomberg, L. DiCaprio, N. Stern, C. Figueres, A. Gore, M. Carney. All of these people have huge carbon footprints, and they fly around the world in private jets to inform us what to do about climate change. They are supported by a whole cadre of senior academics promoting offsetting, negative emissions, geo-engineering, CCS, green growth, etc. These are all an evolution within the system." — Kevin Anderson, Tyndall Centre for Climate Change Research*[568]

568 https://www.counterpunch.org/2019/02/14/capitalisms-ownership-of-global-warming/

## UNDERWAY: THE MONETIZATION OF SOCIAL CAPITAL

André Hoffmann is a Swiss industrialist belonging to one of the wealthiest dynasties in Europe. He served as vice-president of WWF from 2007-2017 and as WWF honorary chair from 1998-2017. He is president of the MAVA Foundation (a key funder[569] of the Natural Capital Coalition) and vice-chairman of the board for Roche,[570] the pharmaceutical and chemical giant founded by his family.[571]

Roche is the world's largest biotech company. It is headquartered in Switzerland and has operations in over 100 countries. As one of the early adopters of the Natural Capital Protocol, the pilot summary report made mention that "an important point raised by the study was the fact that Roche generates considerable **unaccounted for positive social value** from use of their products and other socially responsible activities, **which likely far outweigh any negative environmental impacts**."[572] [Emphasis added]

The above disclosure opens up yet another layer of depravity. If we can assign monetary values to nature – we can assign monetary values to culture as well.

569 https://naturalcapitalproject.stanford.edu/what-is-natural-capital/
570 https://www.roche.com/about/governance/board_of_directors/board_of_directors-hoffmann.htm
571 [Bio: https://www.weforum.org/agenda/authors/andre-s-hoffmann/]
572 https://naturalcapitalcoalition.org/roche-natural-capital-protocol-pilot-summary-report/

Enter the assigning of monetary value to "social capital" in the language of "social capital markets". [Social Capital Markets website: "dedicated to catalyzing world change through market-based solutions."]

NextBillion[573] was launched in May 2005 by the World Resources Institute.[574] The "development through enterprise" project shares an interest in the development of social capital.[575] In 2010, the William Davidson Institute (WDI) at the University of Michigan joined the World Resources Institute as partners in ownership of NextBillion. As of December 4, 2012, NextBillion is managed exclusively by WDI,[576] which is focused on providing private-sector solutions in emerging markets.

> *"Social Capital Markets is Dedicated to Accelerating a New Global Market at the Intersection of Money + Meaning". — Social Capital Markets Website*[577]

The 2017 Social Capital Protocol states that, "integrating approaches between social and natural capital" are driven by the same purpose and based on the same concepts and principles as the Natural Capital Protocol developed by the Natural Capital Coalition. [p. 6]

Although the social capital concept is still in its infancy ["the measurement and valuation of social capital is a relatively new concept"], its goals are clear: "Over the coming years, the Social Capital Protocol initiative will shape and drive collaborative action to achieve four goals." The last goal can best be described as what will be the coup de grâce for the last vestiges of human normality: "Enable companies to capitalize on their implementation of the Social Capital Protocol by ensuring the finance community and capital markets recognize and reward social value creation." [p. 5]

Again, as with the Natural Capital project/coalition, World Resources Institute plays a key role: "These principles align with the current principles of the Natural Capital Protocol, which itself builds on guidance from the Global Reporting Initiative (GRI), the World Resource Institute (WRI)/WBCSD Greenhouse Gas Protocol, and the Climate Disclosure Standards Board (CDSB)." [p. 10]

A new financial system that allows a corporation such as Roche, the world's largest biotech company, to measure and account for positive social value as a means of offsetting "negative environmental impacts" is a great tool indeed. It is little wonder that Hoffman would have invested in its development.

573 https://nextbillion.net/about/
574 https://www.wri.org/our-work/project/nextbillion-development-through-enterprise
575 https://socialcapitalmarkets.net/dt_logos/nextbillion/
576 http://nextbillion.net/blogpost.aspx?blogid=3047
577 https://socialcapitalmarkets.net/

Hoffman also serves as senior advisor at Chatham House[578] and numerous other boards, including the World Economic Forum, the Center for the Fourth Industrial Revolution and SYSTEMIQ.

Here it can be noted that Jeremy Oppenheim, the lead[579] and former programme director of the New Climate Economy,[580] is the founder and managing partner of SYSTEMIQ: "While giving full value to the natural ecosystem, these alternatives need to be economically viable and able to replicate at scale... We envisage successful models rapidly becoming a 'bankable asset class' for regular investors."[581] Oppenheim also serves as chair of the Blended Finance Taskforce.[582] John E. Morton who serves as senior advisor to the Blended Finance Taskforce is a fellow to the European Climate Foundation. Two SYSTEMIQ associates serve as the project leads to the Blended Finance Taskforce.[583] Suffice to say, all roads lead to the Climate Finance Partnership and the New Climate Economy.

André Hoffmann's father, Luc Hoffmann, served on the first international board of the WWF (co-founders include Goddfrey Rockefeller). In addition to his contributions to the founding of WWF, Luc Hoffmann also founded WWF France and WWF Greece. He served as honorary vice-president to WWF until his death in 2016.[584]

In addition to the support provided to the WWF, Luc Hoffmann served as director of Wetlands International, was vice-president of the IUCN (World Union of Nature Conservation) and established the International Bank of Arguin Foundation in Mauritania. This is important to recognize, as in 2013, this project received the "first international payment for marine ecosystem services"[585]

October 29, 2018,[586] WWF Press Release, "WWF Report Reveals Staggering Extent of Human Impact on Planet":

> *"A global deal for nature, similar to the Paris Climate Agreement, can ensure that effective conservation methods continue, and more ambitious goals are set."*

578 https://www.chathamhouse.org/about/governance/andre-hoffmann
579 http://www.ethicalcorp.com/disruptors-how-jeremy-oppenheim-leading-charge-systems-change
580 https://newclimateeconomy.net/blog/authors/jeremy-oppenheim
581 https://www.systemiq.earth/land-use indonesia
582 https://www.blendedfinance.earth/steering-committee
583 https://www.blendedfinance.earth/management-team
584 https://www.wwf.it/?24300
585 [Source: The case of the Banc d'Arguin National Park, Mauritania: https://www.researchgate.net/publication/259138336_First_international_payment_for_marine_ecosystem_services_The_case_of_the_Banc_d'Arguin_National_Park_Mauritania]
586 https://www.worldwildlife.org/press-releases/wwf-report-reveals-staggering-extent-of-human-impact-on-planet

The report states that, "the biggest drivers of current biodiversity loss are overexploitation and agriculture, both linked to continually increasing human consumption." Yet, nowhere does it mention the ecological impacts of militarism. As a collective, we have become so conditioned to this incredible "oversight", that we no longer take notice of its omission. The report draws attention to agriculture, but not to industrial livestock with its staggering ecological impacts coupled with its grotesque cruelty. It draws attention to increasing number of mountain gorillas – just prior to Jane Goodall's promotional support of a fourth industrial revolution in January of 2019, in Davos. A revolution that consequently demands fivefold the minerals and metals[587] we are already using as fast as we can. The very same metals that cause the conflict and resulting death of Congolese men, women and children – and gorillas. Here we can only conclude what those in the Global South have always known: technological "progress" is always intended to serve the West at the expense of what life and what resources remain.

As we peel back the layers, the "New Deal for Nature" is even more egregious than the Green New Deal. Yet, if the NGOs can create enough collective hype around the Green New Deal, in servitude to their funders, the more sinister deal can be brought into legislation without opposition. This bears resemblance to the anti-pipeline NGO campaigns. While Americans were hypnotized by a single pipeline, American business magnate Warren Buffett built a 21st century rail dynasty[588] to ship oil via rail, and the oil continued to flow – only even faster.

587 https://www.mdpi.com/2079-9276/8/1/33/html
588 http://www.theartofannihilation.com/keystone-xl-the-art-of-ngo-discourse-part-i/

## STORYTELLING

> *"... and I will say this to our colleagues from Western civil society — you have definitely sided with a small group of industrialists and their representatives and your representative branches. Nothing more than that. You have become an instrument of your governments." — Lumumba Di-Aping, chief negotiator of the G77, December 11, 2009,[589] COP15*

Above screenshot: In the 2012 David Blood lecture (video), "Breakthrough Capitalism Forum – David Blood", one can view the sponsorship in the background. At the top of the screen, we can identify speakers/sponsors Jeremy Leggett of Solar Century & Carbon Tracker, and Jennifer Morgan of WWF, to name two.
[590]

To demonstrate an example of "storytelling" employed to appease the public and feign opposition to those destroying our planet, we can look at the following Greenpeace International press release: January 25, 2019,[591] "Profit, Not People, Clearly Remains Davos Elites' Priority. As the World Economic Forum in Davos draws to a close, Greenpeace International executive director, Jennifer Morgan, stated:

> *Greenpeace came to Davos looking for moral, business and political leadership, and we did not find it. It is deeply disturbing that, as the world tinkers on the brink of a climate catastrophe, avoid-*

589 https://www.youtube.com/watch?v=zOEG3M7dlDo
590 [Source: http://www.theartofannihilation.com/mckibbens-divestment-tour-brought-to-you-by-wall-street-part-xvi-of-an-investigative-report-beautiful-delusions/]
[See full list of Breakthrough Capitalism partners: http://www.breakthroughcapitalism.com/partners.html]
591 https://www.greenpeace.org/international/press-release/20384/greenpeace-profit-not-people-clearly-remains-davos-elites-priority/

*ing further temperature rise is not at the very centre of all of the meetings of CEOs and world leaders.* ***The solutions are in front of them and they need to prioritise solving this crisis, join the youth who are leading the way forward*** *and thus be on the right side of history.*

*Yesterday there were 32,000 school strike students on the streets of Belgium and today children are taking to the streets of Berlin clamouring for an early coal phase-out.* ***The youth are demanding to be heard, the question is, why isn't the Davos elite responding with the scale and pace required?*** *Short-term business interests and making a greater profit, whatever the cost to others, clearly remains the Davos elites priority.* ***We have no time to waste. In the powerful words of Greta Thunberg,***[592] ***we need to 'get angry, and form that anger into action.'"***

An excerpt from the January 16, 2019[593] press release by Morgan a week prior, as a lead-up[594] to the WEF in Davos, stated:

*"Make no mistake we are in a climate emergency and that emergency must dominate next weeks annual World Economic Forum gathering in Davos.... The Fourth Industrial Revolution could totally reimagine the way we approach solutions to the climate crisis. But only if this revolution is in service of solving climate change."* [595]

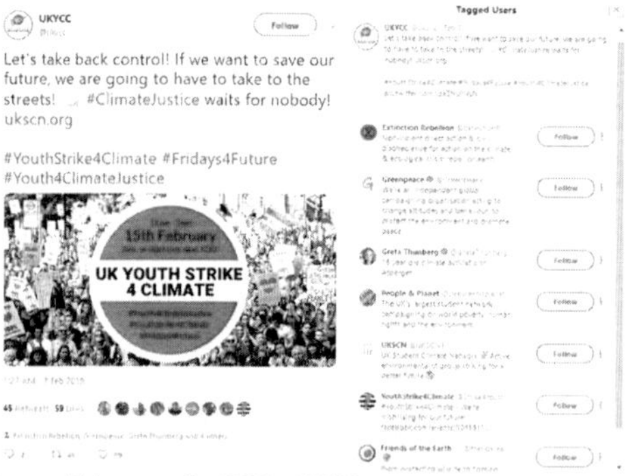


Above: February 7, 2019, UKYCC tweet. Tagged users: Extinction Rebellion, Greenpeace, Greta Thunberg, People & Planet (The UK's largest student network), UKSCN, YouthStrike4Climate and Friends of the Earth

This is very much the green light for the climate strikes in which Greenpeace plays the leading role – in the background.[596]

592 https://www.straitstimes.com/world/time-to-get-angry-teen-climate-activist-says-in-davos

593 https://www.greenpeace.org/international/press-release/20384/greenpeace-profit-not-people-clearly-remains-davos-elites-priority/

594 https://www.greenpeace.org/international/story/20180/hope-is-an-act-of-courage/

595 https://www.greenpeace.org/international/press-release/20295/global-risks-report-climate-emergency-world-economic-forum-davos/

## VOICE FOR THE PLANET

"Voice for the Planet was launched at the World Economic Forum in Davos in 2019 by the **Global Shapers**. The aim, to showcase the growing movement of people around the world calling for a new deal for nature and people: urgent global action to address the current crisis for nature."[597]

The twenty-two organizations supporting the campaign (registered to WWF-UK) include: The Climate Reality Project, World Resources Institute, WWF, Conservation International, the Nature Conservancy and UNDP. [Accessed February 20, 2019][598]

596 https://www.hln.be/de-krant/greenpeace-hielp-initiatiefneemsters~ac0c50d9
597 [Source: Voice for the Planet website: https://voice.ourplanet.com/info/]
598 [Full list: https://voice.ourplanet.com/info/]

## GLOBAL SHAPERS

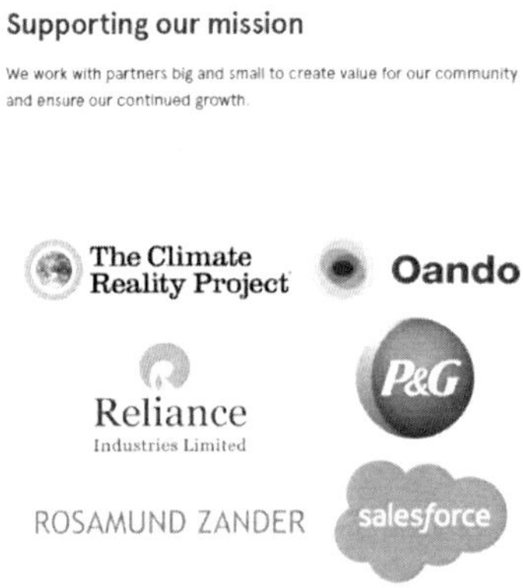


Voice for the Planet leads us to Global Shapers,[599] a global community of "change-makers" – supported by grant and community partners. Founded in 2011 by Klaus Schwab, founder and executive chairman of the World Economic Forum, Global Shapers is a de facto training center for young people under the age of 30 that can shape the world as envisioned by WEF, Al Gore, Jack Ma et al. With more than 7,000 members, the Global Shapers community spans 369 city-based hubs in 171 countries.

Here again we have the youth being trained to destroy their own futures as sacrificial lambs to capitalism.

Serving on the Global Shapers board of directors[600] is David M. Rubenstein, co-founder and co-chief executive officer of the Carlyle Group, and Jack Ma, executive chairman of the Alibaba Group and co-founder of the Breakthrough Energy Coalition.[601]

Partners[602] include: The Climate Reality Project, Coca-Cola, Salesforce, Procter and Gamble,[603] Reliance Industries,[604] Oando,[605] GMR Group, Hanwha Energy Corporation, Rosamund Zander and Yara International.

> *"Lastly, thanks to collaboration with the Climate Reality Project, more than 292 Global Shapers were able to join U.S. Vice President Al Gore at the Climate Reality Leadership Corps training. Global Shapers joined the training that took place in Berlin, Pittsburgh, Mexico City and Los Angeles, as well as during regional SHAPE events, to learn how to lead the global fight for climate solutions." — Global Shapers Annual Report 2017*[606]

599 https://www.globalshapers.org/
600 https://www.globalshapers.org/story
601 http://www.wrongkindofgreen.org/2015/12/07/breakthrough-boondoggle/
602 https://www.globalshapers.org/partnerships
603 https://us.pg.com/
604 http://www.ril.com/
605 https://www.oandoplc.com/
606 https://weforum.box.com/shared/static/sz9as94j6wjlrbsf9lz8xin4b9ftlehu.pdf

The Global Shapers is a grotesque display of corporate malfeasance disguised as good. As an example, under the heading "accelerating change", is the "Coca-Cola Shaping a Better Future Grant Challenge". In 2017 the award was given to the Bogotá Hub in order to "foster peace and reconciliation in conflict-torn areas of Colombia." What the youth enraptured by Global Shapers[607] will not be told is that Coca-Cola has a long and sordid history of murdering union leaders[608] in Columbia.

As discussed in the addendum[609] "The Branding of Alexandria Ocasio-Cortez – By Any Means Necessary" (February 15, 2019), more and more, youth are being recognized and targeted as key drivers of economic growth and influence:

> *"We are becoming increasingly aware that solutions to our global challenges must purposefully engage youth, at all levels – locally, regionally, nationally and globally. This generation has the passion, dynamism and entrepreneurial spirit to shape the future." — Klaus Schwab, founder and executive chairman, World Economic Forum*

This growing body of research[610] is not lost on the power elite that gather annually at Davos, nor on the World Economic Forum that hosts them. Nature Conservancy, January 4, 2019,[611] Ten Groups to Watch in 2019:

> ***"The Revolution Will Be Snapchatted.*** *Forget your John-Hughes-movie stereotypes. Today's teens are civically active, globally minded — and they nearly unanimously agree that we need to do more to address climate change. A study[612] of 31,000 youth from 186 countries found that climate change is their number one concern (surpassing terrorism, poverty and unemployment.) Over 90% agree[613] that science has proven that humans are causing climate change, and nearly 60%[614] plan to work in sustainability.[615]" [Emphasis in original]*

The survey[616] Nature Conservancy highlights has been conducted by Global Shapers. This has nothing to do with goodwill or the well-being of youth. This

607 https://www.globalshapers.org/hubs
608 http://killercoke.org/crimes_colombia.php
609 http://www.wrongkindofgreen.org/2019/02/15/the-branding-of-alexandria-ocasio-cortez-by-any-means-necessary-addendum/
610 https://www.investmentbank.barclays.com/our-insights/generation-z.html
611 https://www.nature.org/en-us/what-we-do/our-insights/perspectives/10-groups-to-watch-in-2019/
612 http://shaperssurvey.org/static/data/WEF_GSC_Annual_Survey_2017.pdf
613 http://shaperssurvey.org/static/data/WEF_GSC_Annual_Survey_2017.pdf
614 https://www.prnewswire.com/in/news-releases/generation-z-wants-more-action-for-a-sustainable-future-reveals-global-research-from-masdar-601450645.html
615 https://www.nature.org/en-us/about-us/who-we-are/how-we-work/youth-engagement/
616 http://shaperssurvey.org/static/data/WEF_GSC_Annual_Survey_2017.pdf

is simple metrics in order to identify, understand, and ultimately exploit, the targeted audience.

In the polling conducted for the 2017 Global Shapers annual survey report, one area of interest is the section concerning "sense of responsibility and responsiveness." When asked who has the greatest responsibility in making the world a better place and thereby the power to address the most important global and local issues, the first choice is 'individuals' (34.2%)". Compare this to 9% of votes feeling the responsibility is with "global and large national companies". ["The top choice is constant regardless of gender, age, regions, Human Development Index, Corruption Perceptions Index or income level."]

In essence, we have youth – many from states whose contribution to climate change is almost nil – who have been convinced to believe their own impact is far greater to ecological devastation than corporations, the economic system itself, or even the global war industry.

Another insight garnered from the survey: "Does the feeling of responsibility translate into any concrete actions? Young people were asked whether they would be willing to change their lifestyle to protect nature and the environment, to which 78.1% responded *yes.*" And this is the primary reason for feigned concern by the world's most powerful capitalists – how the youth can be exploited as consumers.

## MEANWHILE, ON THE "LEADING THE PUBLIC INTO EMERGENCY MODE" FRONT

> *"IF THERE'S NO ACTION before 2012, that's too late. What we do in the next two to three years will determine our future. This is the defining moment." — Rajendra Pachauri, head of the Intergovernmental Panel on Climate Change, Nov. 17, 2007*

> *"We still have a chance to turn things around, though. A major body of research led by The Nature Conservancy shows it is still possible to achieve a sustainable future for people and nature[617]— if we take massive action in the next 10 years. –January 4, 2019[618]*

Meanwhile, in terms of the authorities in the "Leading the Public into Emergency Mode" front, we have the very same groups that brought us into the fold of the 2009 TckTckTck campaign for COP15 ("a movement that consumers, ad-

617 https://www.nature.org/en-us/what-we-do/our-insights/perspectives/the-science-of-sustainability/
618 https://www.nature.org/en-us/what-we-do/our-insights/perspectives/10-groups-to-watch-in-2019/

vertisers and the media would use and exploit") – that were then able to "herd the cats" for the People's Climate March, orchestrated in 2014 – and are now tasked with mobilizing the populace again for the final crescendo, requiring even larger unprecedented numbers. Hence, we have headlines such as "The Human Survival Summit: The Next Wave Of Climate Change Protests Is Coming – Greenpeace and Amnesty International unite in push for greater civil disobedience." [January 25, 2019][619]

The irony here is that both Greenpeace and TckTckTck threw all the world's most vulnerable citizens under the bus[620] in 2009 during the tenure of Kumi Naidoo who served as executive director of both organizations. Today, a decade later, Naidoo now leads Amnesty International as its secretary-general. In 2011, Amnesty International, by utilizing the behavioural economics of hatred, was instrumental[621] in leading the illegal war on the sovereign nation of Libya – Libya being the most prosperous country in Africa under the leadership of Libyan revolutionary Muammar Gaddafi.[622] Libya quickly became a war-torn nation in a permanent state of chaos as hundreds of thousands of citizens perished (and continue to do so to this day). Yet, the elite institutions and oligarchs that finance it, control it and wield it as a weapon in the service of imperialism and patriarchy, would like you to believe that they actually have concern about the climate and human rights:

> *"Greenpeace International, which has traditionally focused on environmental issues, and Amnesty International, which has concentrated on human rights, are co-launching a Summit for Human Survival later this year to encourage nonviolent protests and other interventions that force greater action on climate change.*
>
> *The idea of the Summit, said Naidoo, is not for it to dictate or try to coordinate centralized actions but rather to unite individuals and organizations so that they can collaborate in pushing for change. He pointed to new forms of protest such as the Extinction Rebellion movement,[623] one of the many youth-driven civil disobedience movements focused on climate change. It began in the U.K. and is now launching chapters across the globe, including in the United States. Naidoo added that big international NGOs*

619 https://www.huffingtonpost.co.uk/entry/the-human-survival-summit-the-next-wave-of-climate-change-protests-is-coming_us_5c4b4d8be4b0e1872d4368f4
620 http://www.theartofannihilation.com/the-most-important-cop-briefings-that-no-one-ever-heard-truth-lies-racism-omnicide/
621 https://www.youtube.com/watch?v=opmQIkSvYgY
622 https://www.africanexponent.com/post/8136-nelson-mandelas-friendship-with-gaddafi-that-irritated-the-west
623 https://www.huffingtonpost.com/entry/sunrise-movement-climate-chnage-direct-action-fossil-fuels_us_5c122a7ae4b002a46c143f73

*aren't organizing this mobilization and that this sort of decentralization should be encouraged."*

And this too is a lie.

Having initially intended to write extensively in this segment about Extinction Rebellion, the need to do so is no longer paramount. It suffices to point out the fact that The Climate Mobilization NGO (whose founder is the author of the aforementioned paper "Leading the Public into Emergency Mode," which collaborates with 350.org, The Leap and many others) has been working with Extinction Rebellion since at least last September.[624] This reveals why the Extinction Rebellion group was catapulted into international super stardom by The Guardian et al while far greater actions by land defenders in the Global South go ignored for eternity.

If that is not sufficient substantiation for some readers, it is fact that 350.org, Avaaz, Friends of the Earth and Greenpeace have all been in dialogue with the Extinction Rebellion co-founders, whom, with The Climate Mobilization, are very much in favour of such collaboration. [Interview with ER co-founders by The Climate Mobilization founder, December 6, 2018]:[625]

> ***Bradbrook:*** *"...at the start of this campaign in back in early October we did an occupation of Greenpeace's offices. It was very friendly. We took cake and flowers and everybody hid the horns from Roger so it couldn't go around blowing the horns because we wanted to keep it really lovely...*
>
> ***We are having conversations with organizations, [] conversation with [] some of the [] bigger online platforms even than 350.org****. It's always an important balance to figure out how you have a relationship with any kind of NGO so that there's not big compromises being asked for, and watch this space on that front. I think I shouldn't pre-announce things on here that aren't being agreed yet with everybody else, but we yeah we are definitely talking to other organizations. More tricky than you think, quite often."*
>
> ***Hallam:*** *"...so this is a very serious sort of proposition that we're putting to some of the [] NGOs which are, I think a lot of the peo-*

624 Gregory Schwedock, NY, NY, USA is the director of digital organizing for the Climate Mobilization Project (2014-present). He identifies himself as coordinator for Extinction Rebellion from September 2018 – present. [Source: LinkedIn]

625 https://youtu.be/8AUFeT_QWwA?t=3995

*ple in the NGOs know this as well. I mean a lot of people know what's coming and I think this opens up a really interesting space in progressive culture in the countries we're in. For the first time for a generation or two is to basically create a united front as it were people working together on a common agenda and I've been personally really surprised by how open some of the people have been at* ***Greenpeace and Avaaz and various other organizations*** *to the notion that, yes, we need to have as mass participation in civil disobedience and that's going to be the future, we've run out of other options."*

The NGO relationships formed with Extinction Rebellion explain the deliberately vague three demands behind the Extinction Rebellion "movement" – a vagueness that goes largely unnoticed – while one particular demand is as clear as the light of day. While imperialism, capitalism and militarism – the main drivers of ecological devastation and climate change are nowhere to be found, there is something that is found buried in the FAQ section:[626]

Question: "WHY HAVEN'T YOU GOT MORE TANGIBLE WINNABLE STEPPING STONE GOALS THAT WOULD BUILD MORAL [SIC] AS YOU WIN?"

Extinction Rebellion: "We have. We say the Government must reverse current policies inconsistent with acknowledging the climate emergency – there is much to be achieved there. For example banning fracking and dropping plans for a third runway at Heathrow. And reversing their decision to crush renewable energy investment while doubling down on fossil fuels. **A massive Green New Deal is absolutely vital, possible and necessary."**

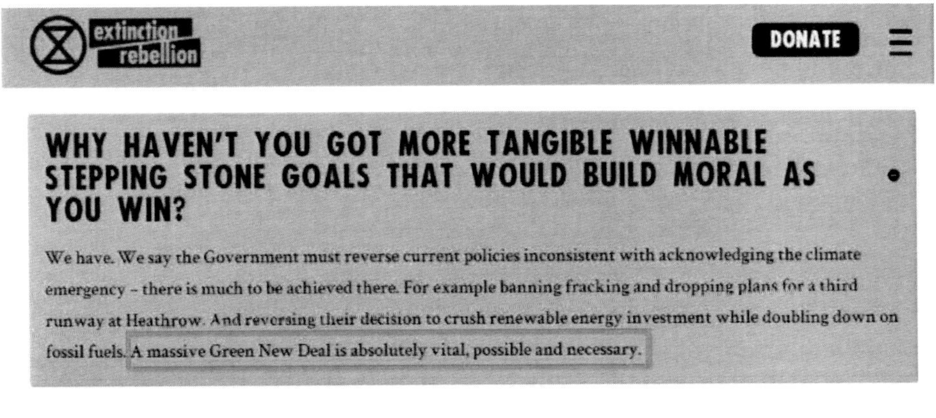


626 https://rebellion.earth/faqs/

Here, one must ask why a UK group would identify a US campaign[627] as a primary focal point of its demands. The answer is that, not only were US NGOs already officially involved with Extinction Rebellion as early as September 2018 while simultaneously being aggressive proponents of the Green New Deal, but even more importantly, these NGOs, at the bequest of their benefactors, also had global designs[628] for Green New Deals. The New Deal For Nature would be helped along after popularizing the language of "new deal" in order to mask its ugly intent. The New Deal for Nature, saturated with holistic linguistics and emotive hooks,[629] lies in the dark shadows of the Green New Deal and climate strikes – waiting.

In the October 31, 2018[630] article covering the very first Extinction Rebellion action, published by the aforementioned DeSmogBlog, a reference to a "new deal for nature" goes undetected:

> *"Extinction Rebellion's declaration of rebellion comes a day after a report by the WWF[631] found that many species' populations have declined on average by 60 percent between 1970 and 2014 largely due to human activity.*
>
> *The report said: 'Decision makers at every level need to make the right political, financial and consumer choices to achieve the vision that humanity and nature thrive in harmony on our only planet.'*
>
> *The WWF called for* ***'a new global deal for nature and people'*** *to halt wildlife decline, tackle deforestation, climate change and plastic pollution and is backed by 'concrete commitments from global leaders and businesses.'"*

The fact that Extinction Rebellion does not include capitalism, imperialism or militarism – the primary drivers of the ecological assault against the Earth, in conjunction with the omission of other underlying structural causes, has raised important questions about whether or not this vehicle can perhaps still be utilized to organize and build community.

Here, the question must be, why would we choose to lend our name to strengthen a BRAND that cites "a massive new deal is absolutely vital," yet de-

627 https://www.greanvillepost.com/2019/02/24/scurrying-fascist-cockroaches/
628 https://act.350.org/signup/GND-canada/
629 https://twitter.com/hashtag/NewDealforNature?src=hash
630 https://www.desmog.co.uk/2018/10/31/protesters-arrested-outside-parliament-extinction-rebellion-against-climate-inaction
631 https://www.wwf.org.uk/updates/living-planet-report-2018

liberately omits the fact that stopping capitalism, imperialism and militarism and other forms of oppression that are just as vital. This is worse than an oversight. It is a disgrace. Even more tragic is the fact that collectively we have been conditioned to such an extent, we are no longer even cognizant of such blatant hypocrisies.

As an ongoing coup against the sovereign state of Venezuela led by the US and Canada accelerates – Extinction Rebellion fails to mobilize their groups, now international in scope. They not only fail to mobilize, they fail to speak of it. With its arms opened to imperialist NGOs such as Avaaz and Amnesty International, the writing was already on the wall before the first action took place.

Adding to this, is the fact that Extinction Rebellion is yet another group that chooses to stay absolutely silent on the commodification and objectification of nature – another tell-tale warning sign.

We must lend our support and engage in small but connected resistance groups[632] that work together to tear down the structures oppressing not only ourselves – but foremost, our brothers and sisters in the Global South. This means crushing the drivers of imperialism.[633]

## THE LAST VESTIGES OF ETHICS AND THE CORPORATE CAPTURE OF NATURE

This series has disclosed very ugly truths. It is our ethical and moral duty to share this knowledge. Only then, can the tide turn. The era of "green shaming" must come to an end.[634] It has been used as a weapon to ensure our silence for long enough.

This is 350.org – born out of The Rockefeller Foundation. This is Avaaz – an instrument of empire – up to its neck in the blood of Libyan and Syrian men, women and children while campaigning for climate action as it creates acquiescence for wars. This is Greenpeace that cited the world must not exceed a global temperature increase of 1°C in 1997[635] only to demand a full 2°C in 2009. This is Friends of the Earth, who has served on the board of Ceres, since its inception – that also cited 1°C in 2001[636] as the global temperature that the

632 http://www.theburningspear.com/about/uhuru-movement

633 [Essential reading for youth: CHE GUEVARA TALKS TO YOUNG PEOPLE. (http://www.kwela.com/Books/19432) "Between 1959 and 1964, freedom fighter Che Guevara delivered a number of speeches to youth groups and students to inspire and educate them about the revolution. This is a collection of these speeches – a collection of thought as iconic as Che Guevara's image. He remains a hero to many, and represents a form of socialism that is hard to deny."]
[Download: https://www.academia.edu/38435005/Che_Guevara_Talks_To_Young_People]

634 [Trust Nothing – John Steppling: https://www.counterpunch.org/2019/02/01/trust-nothing/]

635 https://www.academia.edu/3880272/Greenpeace_International_Cites_Maximum_1C_UNAGGG_October_1_1997

636 https://www.academia.edu/3880161/Friends_of_the_Earth_Finland_Cites_Maximum_1C_UNAGGG_March_15_2001

Earth must not exceed. This is a cabal that has placed capital and corporate interests over environmental protection and Indigenous rights – time and time again.

> *"Many of you equally, and I will say this, and I would have never thought that one day I will accuse a civil society of such a thing. Dividing the G77, or helping divide the G77, is simply something that should be left to the CIAs, the KGBs and the rest [not the NGOs]. — Lumumba Di-Aping, chief negotiator of the G77, December 11, 2009,*[637] *COP15*

Clive L. Spash, WU Vienna University of Economics and Business, Vienna, Austria, writes: "The Paris Agreement signifies commitment to sustained industrial growth, risk management over disaster prevention, and future inventions and technology as saviour. The primary commitment of the international community is to maintain the current social and economic system. The result is denial that tackling GHG emissions is incompatible with sustained economic growth. The reality is that Nation States and international corporations are engaged in an unremitting and ongoing expansion of fossil fuel energy exploration, extraction and combustion, and the construction of related infrastructure for production and consumption. The targets and promises of the Paris Agreement bear no relationship to biophysical or social and economic reality." [This Changes Nothing: The Paris Agreement to Ignore Reality, Globalizations, 2016 Vol. 13, No. 6, 928–933][638]

Thunberg has stated repeatedly that her strike will continue "until Sweden is aligned with the Paris Agreement." Therefore, by her own statements, this is the singular, overall purpose and goal of the strikes, now global in scale. A Paris Agreement that unlocks everything which has been disclosed in painstaking detail within this series.

On February 21, 2019,[639] the European Commission[640] was the latest to embrace and promote Thunberg: "The teenager opened a European Commission event[641] in front of President Jean-Claude Juncker where she told politicians to stop 'sweeping their mess under the carpet for our generation to clean up.'" Here again, Thunberg's demands, on behalf of the youth participating in the climate strikes, are identified:

637 https://www.youtube.com/watch?v=zOEG3M7dlDo
638 https://www.clivespash.org/wp-content/uploads/2015/04/2016-Spash-This-Changes-Nothing.pdf
639 https://youtu.be/sVeYOPJZ8oc
640 https://ec.europa.eu/commission/index_en
641 https://www.eu-events.eu/12865-civil-society-for-reunaissance.html

*"We want you to **follow the Paris agreement** and the IPCC reports **we don't have any other manifests or demands**. Just unite behind the science. That is our demand."* [642]

Here we have three key players of capitalist hegemony, the World Bank, the World Economic Forum and the European Commission – all promoting Thunberg in unprecedented fashion. Institutions housing individuals that systematically pillage the planet in exchange for economic growth, power and profits have been magically moved to protect the planet.

February 23, 2019: "De Franse president Macron ontving het Zweedse klimaatmeisje Greta Thunberg (rechts naar Macron) en een delegatie van Youth for Climate, onder wie Anuna De Wever (tweede van rechts) en Kyra Gantois (eerste van links)." [643]

What is unbeknownst to the populace is the fact that all three of these institutions are founding architects/partners of the Climate Finance Partnership which is aligned with the Blended Finance Taskforce.[644] The Climate Finance Partnership[645] was formed under the leadership of French President Em-

642 https://youtu.be/sVeYOPJZ8oc
643 https://www.hln.be/nieuws/buitenland/macron-ontvangt-greta-thunberg-anuna-de-wever-en-kyra-gantois-in-het-elysee-het-was-een-positieve-ontmoeting~aa31b354/
644 https://www.blendedfinance.earth/steering-committee
645 https://europeanclimate.org/governments-and-philanthropies-announce-ground-breaking-partnership-with-blackrock-to-mobilize-and-deploy-climate-finance-at-scale/

manuel Macron who announced the partnership on September 26, 2018 at the One Planet Summit[646] held in New York. Partners[647] of the Climate Finance Partnership include the governments of France and Germany. The One Planet Summit is organized by the Government of France jointly with the UN, the World Bank Group and Bloomberg Philanthropies.[648]

The Climate Finance Partnership was created in order to propel forward the New Climate Economy.[649] Both being key vehicles to unlock the 100 trillion dollars identified in pension funds while simultaneously implementing the economic valuation and payment for environmental services (payments for ecosystems services) hidden within the Sustainable Development Goals. The privatization of nature will transform global finance. Those most responsible for the destruction will be assigned as the new "stewards of national natural capital."[650]

One can only hope that this series has finally divulged once and for all who and what such powerful NGOs represent: oligarchs, corporate finance and capital. The NGOs at the helm of non-profit industrial complex must be recognized as the world's most powerful lobbying arm for green technology. This comes at the expense of nature, not for the protection of nature. Again, reality turned on its head. This is why the non-profit industrial complex must be starved out of commission – by withdrawing our consent. Up to this point its power stems from its false claim of representing civil society. We must make it clear that it does not.

We have planetary boundaries that we must live within if life on Earth is to continue in some shape or form. These boundaries are non-negotiable. We can lie to ourselves all we want, in all of our anthropocentric glory, but it won't change the reality. We can paint it green,[651] we can share our illusions in glossy brochures and make them go viral on shiny screens – the biosphere does not give a flying fuck. If our society was actually sane, we would recognize these said "solutions" as delusions – but sadly that is not the case. Disconnected from nature – and more and more, disconnected from each other – we are lost.

Nature doesn't deal.

---

646 https://www.oneplanetsummit.fr/en
647 https://europeanclimate.org/governments-and-philanthropies-announce-ground-breaking-partnership-with-blackrock-to-mobilize-and-deploy-climate-finance-at-scale/
648 http://sdg.iisd.org/events/one-planet-summit/
649 https://newclimateeconomy.net/
650 http://www.theartofannihilation.com/mckibbens-divestment-tour-brought-to-you-by-wall-street-part-xiii-the-increasing-vogue-for-capitalist-friendly-climate-discourse/
651 https://www.corporateknights.com/channels/responsible-investing/clean-transition-bonds-unlock-1t-oil-sands-opportunities-15403846/

*"And that's the real question facing the white activists today. Can they tear down the institutions that have put us all in the trick bag we've been into for the last hundreds of years?" — Black Power by Stokely Carmichael, 1966*

We can end this grim instalment by reflecting upon what Indian author Arundhati Roy so articulately summarized almost fifteen years ago on August 16, 2004: "The NGO-ization of resistance."[652] We can say that tragically, yet unequivocally, the NGO-ization of resistance in the West is a *fait accompli.*

European Commission President Jean-Claude Juncker kissing the hand of Greta Thunberg at a conference in Brussels, Belgium February 21, 2019. REUTERS/Yves Herman

652 https://youtu.be/rgYaZAUzwuY

[Cory Morningstar is an independent investigative journalist, writer and environmental activist, focusing on global ecological collapse and political analysis of the non-profit industrial complex. She resides in Canada. Her recent writings can be found on Wrong Kind of Green,[653] The Art of Annihilation[654] and Counterpunch.[655] Her writing has also been published by Bolivia Rising[656] and Cambio,[657] the official newspaper of the Plurinational State of Bolivia. You can support her independent journalism via Patreon.[658]]

[Forrest Palmer is an electrical engineer residing in Texas. He is a part-time blogger and writer and can be found on Facebook. You may reach him at forrest_palmer@yahoo.com.]

[Boris Forkel is a radical environmentalist, social rights activist and subsistence farmer. The books he publishes with his press BabylonApocalypse[659] inspire and encourage dissidents to break through an increasingly narrow public discourse and spread the seeds of decisive resistance and radical social change.]

653 http://www.wrongkindofgreen.org/
654 http://theartofannihilation.com/
655 http://www.counterpunch.org/
656 http://boliviarising.blogspot.ca/
657 http://www.cambio.bo/
658 https://www.patreon.com/CoryMorningstar
659 http://babylonapocalypse.org